YORK NOTES

General Editors: Professor A. ʃeffares (*University of Stirling*) & Professor Suheil Bushrui (*American University of Beirut*)

Geoffrey Chaucer

THE CLERK'S TALE

Notes by Colin Wilcockson

MA (OXFORD)
Fellow and Director of Studies in English, Pembroke College, Cambridge

LONGMAN
YORK PRESS

Acknowledgement

The section '"Thou" and "Ye"', under 'The language of the *Clerk's Tale*', on pp. 44–6, is an abbreviated version of Colin Wilcockson's, '"Thou" and "Ye" in Chaucer's *Clerk's Tale*', *Use of English*, Vol.31, No.3, Summer 1980, pp. 37–43. Permission to publish this shortened version has kindly been given by the Scottish Academic Press.

YORK PRESS
Immeuble Esseily, Place Riad Solh, Beirut.

LONGMAN GROUP UK LIMITED
Longman House, Burnt Mill, Harlow,
Essex CM20 2JE, England
and Associated Companies throughout the World

© Librairie du Liban 1987

First published 1987

ISBN 0-582-79290-8

Produced by Longman Group (FE) Ltd
Printed in Hong Kong

Contents

Part 1

Introduction

Chaucer's life

External evidence about Chaucer's life is found in a number of official records relating to payments made to him, legal transactions in which he was involved, and so on. There are, however, periods of his life about which we know nothing. Internal evidence is found in what Chaucer says about himself in his own works: some of this is more or less factual about his work as an accountant or refers to poems he has written previously. It is instinctive for a reader to want to infer from his writings something about the character of the poet, and indeed Chaucer depicts himself as shy, plump, short, apologetic and incompetent. So obviously facetious is the tone of his self-references that we are little further forward, and we are left to speculate about the nature of the man from the attitudes that seem inherent in the works. In the last analysis this exercise remains, of course, nothing but speculation.

Chaucer was born around 1340 and died in 1400. He thus lived in the reigns of Edward III (1327–77), Richard II (1377–99) and in the first year of the reign of Henry IV, who had deposed Richard. These were turbulent times of protracted wars with France, of court factions and regicide, of the Peasants' Revolt (1381) and of the devastating plague, the Black Death, which swept through Europe, reaching England in 1348, and erupted in appalling epidemics throughout and beyond the rest of Chaucer's life.

Chaucer's father was a London vintner and Geoffrey was probably born in the family house in Thames Street. By the time he was seventeen, he was a page in the household of the Countess of Ulster, wife of the Duke of Clarence. He was taken prisoner while on military service in France, and Edward III contributed a substantial sum towards his ransom. He married Philippa, a lady-in-waiting to the queen. Philippa's sister, Katherine, was the mistress, and eventually the wife, of John of Gaunt.

Gaunt, Duke of Lancaster and fourth son of Edward III, was probably the most powerful baron in the land. It appears that Chaucer may have been favoured by Gaunt well before they were related by marriage. Gaunt's first wife, Blanche of Lancaster, died in 1369, and Chaucer's earliest known poem, the *Book of the Duchess*, commemorates her death and presents a highly complimentary picture of Gaunt as a mourning knight.

Between 1370 and 1378, Chaucer was employed on diplomatic missions on the Continent, notably in France and Italy. It is probable that in this way he became acquainted with the works of the Italian writers Dante (1265–1321), Boccaccio (1315?–75) and Petrarch (1304–74).

From 1374 onwards, Chaucer held a number of responsible administrative posts, including that of comptroller of wools and hides (the production of which was the single most important English industry of the day) in the port of London. He writes of this period with amusing self-deprecation in the *House of Fame*, where an eagle, carrying Chaucer through the sky, describes him as a man so occupied with his daily work and evening reading and writing that he scarcely notices the life at his very door:

> thou wolt make
> A-nyght ful ofte thyn hed to ake
> In thy studye, so thou writest...
> But of thy verray neyghebores,
> That duellen* almost at thy dores,
> Thou herist* neyther that ne this;
> For when thy labour doon al ys,
> And hast mad alle thy rekenynges,
> In stede of reste and newe thynges,
> Thou goost hom to thy hous anoon*;
> And, also domb* as any stoon*,
> Thou sittest at another book
> Tyl fully daswed* is thy look...

(*House of Fame*, lines 631–58)

In spite of the political upheavals of the time, with their dangerously conflicting allegiances, Chaucer succeeded in retaining the favours of the great. He received, albeit with interruptions, emoluments from the three monarchs whom he served, and also a life pension from Gaunt. Such payments were for his services as courtier and administrator, and, no doubt, in recognition of his genius as court poet.

Chaucer died in 1400, and was buried in Westminster Abbey.

Chaucer's works

Chaucer's earlier works were strongly influenced by his reading of the literature of France, particularly the thirteenth-century allegorical dream-poem, the *Roman de la Rose*, and the works of the fourteenth-century poet and composer Guillaume de Machaut. The elegiac poem,

---

* *duellen*, dwell; *herist*, hearest; *anoon*, at once; *also domb*, as dumb; *stoon*, stone; *daswed*, dazed.

the *Book of the Duchess*, commemorating the death of Blanche of Lancaster, wife of John of Gaunt, belongs to this period. French influence is visible not only in the subject matter, but also in many closely translated passages; more pervasively, there is a subtle blend of French and native English traditions. In this poem, comedy and tragedy intermingle, endowing the work with a bitter-sweet poignancy which is evident in much of Chaucer's later writing. In it, too, Chaucer presents the poet-narrator as a naïf innocent, scarcely aware of the significance of the wonderful dream-vision which is the subject of his poem. This self-mockery (Machaut had employed a similarly comic self-presentation in his poems) is developed throughout Chaucer's works, as in the description of Chaucer in the *House of Fame* (quoted on p. 6) and continuing into the *Canterbury Tales*. There, he depicts himself as a shy little man whose poetic contribution to the tale-telling competition, *Sir Thopas*, is so boring that it is cut short by Harry Bailly, the host, much to the indignation of the pilgrim Chaucer.

The next works after the *Book of the Duchess* exhibit Italian influence. Chief among these are the *House of Fame* and the *Parliament of Fowls* and, soon afterwards, Chaucer's greatest tragic work, *Troilus and Criseyde*, whose main source is Boccaccio's poem *Il Filostrato*.

The work for which Chaucer is best known, however, is the *Canterbury Tales*, a vast fragment (only twenty-four of the proposed hundred and twenty tales were actually written) and it is likely that some of the tales were written early and adapted to fit the later collection. The framework story is that of a company of about thirty pilgrims setting out from a London inn (of which Harry Bailly is the host) to the shrine of St Thomas Becket in Canterbury Cathedral. They undertake to tell two stories each on the way, and two more on the homeward journey, in a light-hearted competition to win a free supper at Harry Bailly's inn.

The idea of a series of stories set in the framework of an overall story had been used by Boccaccio in the *Decameron* (see pp. 34–6) and by Chaucer's friend John Gower in the *Confessio Amantis*. But Chaucer's pilgrimage framework allows him a wide range through the social hierarchy not possible in the collections of Boccaccio and Gower. Tough, coarse characters, such as the Miller, tell racy fabliaux; others more refined, such as the Franklin and the Knight, tell stories of courtly love and chivalric splendour; preachers, such as the Parson, the Nun's Priest and the Pardoner, tell sermon tales, and so on. Thus almost the whole gamut of medieval narrative genres can be represented, juxtaposed, even satirising and parodying each other (just as the *Miller's Tale* comically mirrors the *Knight's Tale*), and yet be contained within the overall framework story.

The *Canterbury Tales* is prefaced by the *General Prologue* in which thumbnail sketches are given of the pilgrims. Some of these are expanded and developed in the link passages between the tales (see pp. 38–40); some of the tales are projections of the characters of their narrators; some mock other pilgrims. Thus there is a complex interweaving of the separate tales and the framework story.

Allegory was a common mode in the Middle Ages and many of Chaucer's characters are 'types': the fat Monk who even swears by using gastronomic oaths (a monastic regulation was 'not worth an oyster', he 'didn't give a plucked chicken' for a patristic text) would have been recognisable as a close relation of the Deadly Sin of Gluttony, and the red-stockinged Alison of Bath as akin to Lechery. Yet Chaucer endows these types with personal quirks that give them individuality, and it is for this ability to see into the obscure corners of personality that he has been particularly admired. The poet Dryden, in an essay published in 1700, is particularly impressed by this ageless quality of Chaucer's depiction of unchanging human nature:

> He must have been a man of a most wonderful comprehensive nature, because, as has been truly observed of him, he has taken into the compass of his *Canterbury Tales* the various manners and humours (as we now call them) of the whole English nation in his age. Not a single character has escaped from him. All his pilgrims are severally distinguished from each other; and not only in their inclinations, but in their very phisiognomies and persons . . . The matter and manner of their tales, and of their telling, are so suited that each of them would be improper in any other mouth . . . We have our fore-fathers and great grand-dames all before us, as they were in Chaucer's days; their general characters are still remaining in mankind . . . for mankind is ever the same.*

The relationship between the Clerk and the tale he tells is discussed elsewhere (pp. 38–40). Below is quoted his character sketch from the *General Prologue*:

> A CLERK ther was of Oxenford also,
> That unto logyk hadde longe ygo†.
> As leene was his hors as is a rake,
> And he nas nat right fat, I undertake†.
> But looked holwe, and therto sobrely†.
> Ful thredbare was his overeste courtepy†;

---

* John Dryden, *Preface to Fables Ancient and Modern*, 1700; the relevant passage appears in J.J. Anderson (ed.), Chaucer, *The Canterbury Tales*, Casebook Series, Macmillan, London, 1977, pp. 20–32.
† *unto logyk hadde longe ygo*, had studied a long time; *undertake*, guarantee; *holwe, and therto sobrely*, hollow, and moreover gravely so; *overeste courtepy*, upper shortcoat;

For he hadde geten hym yet no benefice*,
Ne was so worldly for to have office*.
For hym was levere* have at his beddes heed*
Twenty bookes, clad* in blak or reed,
Of Aristotle and his philosophie,
Than robes riche, or fithele*, or gay sautrie*.
But al be that he was a philosophre*,
Yet hadde he but litel gold in cofre*;
But al that he myghte of his freendes* hente*,
On bookes and on lernynge he it spente,
And bisily gan for the soules preye
Of hem that yaf* hym wherwith to scoleye*.
Of studie took he moost cure* and moost heede.
Noght o* word spak he moore than was neede,
And that was seyd in forme and reverence*,
And short and quyk* and ful of hy sentence*;
Sownynge* in moral vertu* was his speche,
And gladly wolde he lerne and gladly teche.

(*General Prologue*, lines 285–308)

Many of the general remarks in this section on Chaucer's works have specific application to the Clerk and his tale – to the link between teller and tale, to the inter-relationships between the *Clerk's Tale* and other tales and to the allegorical nature of the story.

A note on the text

The *Canterbury Tales* survive in some ninety manuscripts and early printed versions – some of which are fragmentary – from the fifteenth and sixteenth centuries. They give different parts of the tales in different orders, and have a number of variant readings. However, the text of the *Clerk's Tale* is not greatly in dispute. This commentary is based on the text of F.N. Robinson, *The Complete Works of Geoffrey Chaucer*, second edition, Oxford University Press, Oxford, 1957.

---

* *benefice*, Church living; *office*, secular employment; *For hym was levere*, he preferred to; *his beddes heed*, the head of his bed; *clad*, bound; *fithele*, violin; *sautrie*, psaltery (musical instrument); *philosophre*, 'philosopher' was sometimes a nickname for 'alchemist'; *cofre*, coffer; *freendes*, relations; *hente*, receive; *yaf*, gave; *wherwith to scoleye*, funds to study; *cure*, care; *o*, one; *forme and reverence*, formality and respect; *quyk*, intelligent; *hy sentence*, deep meaning; *Sownynge*, tending to; *moral vertu*, morality.

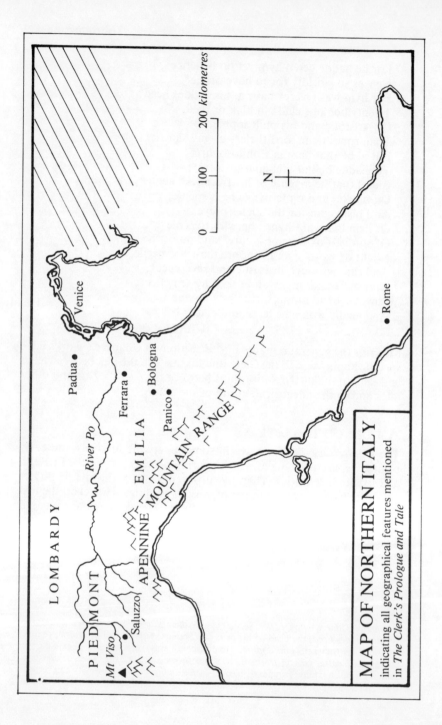

MAP OF NORTHERN ITALY

indicating all geographical features mentioned in *The Clerk's Prologue and Tale*

LOMBARDY

PIEDMONT

Mt Viso ▲

Saluzzo

River Po

EMILIA

APENNINE MOUNTAIN RANGE

Padua ●

Ferrara ●

Bologna ●

Panico ●

Venice

Rome ●

N

0   100   200 *kilometres*

Part 2

Summaries

of the CLERK'S TALE

A general summary

The outline of the story of Grisildis is as follows: Walter, an Italian nobleman, rules over the prosperous estate of Saluzzo. He is handsome and courteous, but his people are unhappy because he is unmarried and they fear that, in the event of his death, the governance of the estate will pass to an unknown marquis instead of to his direct heir. They beg him to marry. Walter agrees to their request, asking in return that they will unquestioningly recognise as their lady whomsoever he may choose. A day for the wedding is arranged.

A beautiful and virtuous peasant girl, Grisildis, lives with her poor father in a nearby village which forms part of Walter's estate. Their lives are hard. Frequently, when out hunting, Walter has observed the girl and admired her goodness, and he determines that Grisildis will be his bride. Walter has a gown and jewels prepared for her and, on the day appointed for the wedding, he rides to the village. Meanwhile, Grisildis, ignorant of his intentions, hurries her work so that she will be able to watch the wedding procession. As she enters her house, Walter comes to her and asks to speak to her father, Janicula, and when he is fetched Walter asks permission to marry Grisildis. The astonished Janicula agrees, and Walter proposes to Grisildis, warning her that he will require absolute obedience from her if she marries him. She assents, is dressed in the fine clothes and the wedding takes place. Grisildis is universally loved and admired for her tact, gentleness and virtue.

A daughter is born to the couple. Walter decides to test Grisildis. He tells her that the people despise her peasant origins and sends an official to Grisildis demanding the baby girl, apparently to kill her. Grisildis, though distressed, does not resist her husband's command. Walter is told of her reaction. The girl is taken to Bologna to be cared for by Walter's sister.

Four years later, Grisildis gives birth to a son. When the child is two years old Walter tells Grisildis that the same fate that befell her daughter must befall the son, because, he says, his people do not want a grandson of Janicula eventually to become the Marquis. Grisildis replies that above all things she desires to be subservient to Walter's will. Walter is privately amazed at her patience and obedience, but when the people hear of his behaviour, they are shocked. When the daughter is twelve, Walter procures counterfeit letters from the Vatican stating that, to keep peace between himself and his people, he has permission to divorce Grisildis. He sends letters to his sister and her husband asking them to proclaim that the young girl in their care is to marry the Marquis of Saluzzo and requesting that she and her brother should come in grand procession to Saluzzo. Walter tells Grisildis of his impending wedding and she receives the news patiently, asking only that her simple peasant dress be returned to her so that she will not be forced to return home naked. Shortly afterwards, Walter summons Grisildis to the palace, asking her to take charge of the arrangements so that everything is fit to receive his new bride. She meekly and willingly agrees.

When the young girl arrives for her wedding, some of the people, much impressed by her beauty, are glad that they are to have a new marchioness. Grisildis, when asked by Walter whether she admires the young lady, replies that she does but begs Walter to treat her more gently than he had treated her. At this point, Walter explains all to Grisildis, telling her that the children are hers and that his actions had been only to test her patience. Grisildis is overcome with joy. They continue in great happiness for the rest of their lives.

The Clerk explains that the moral of the story is not that all wives should behave like Grisildis, but rather that the tale is an allegory of our proper relationship with God: though we may appear to be unfairly treated in life, our proper duty is to take all patiently because we are ignorant of the ultimate will of God who often tests our steadfastness.

Detailed summaries

The Prologue to the Clerk's Tale (lines 1–56)

The bluff landlord of the Tabard Inn in Eastcheap, London, from which the pilgrims in the *Canterbury Tales* set out on their journey to Canterbury, is described in the *General Prologue* (lines 751–7). He is a big man, outspoken and cheerful, in strong contrast to the Oxford scholar. Of the Clerk we learn (*General Prologue*, lines 285–308) that he did not speak a single word unless there was something of importance to say. In the *Prologue to the Clerk's Tale* the Host teases the Clerk for his shyness and for his preoccupation, evidently with some philosophical problem. He asks him to tell a story that is not too serious in subject matter or too ornate in style. The Clerk acknowledges Harry Bailly's authority and undertakes to tell a tale which he has learnt from the great Italian writer Francis Petrarch. Perhaps as a concession to the Host, he promises to omit Petrarch's highly rhetorical introductory passage describing the area where the tale is set, and says that he will, instead, launch immediately into the story.

NOTES AND GLOSSARY:

bord:	table. In this case banqueting table at a wedding. Notice how the theme of marriage is immediately suggested
sophyme:	a superficially persuasive argument which is, however, logically faulty
Salomon:	Solomon, son of David and Bathsheba, King of Israel (974?–937? BC). The reference is to Ecclesiastes 3:1
as beth:	be! The construction '*as* + imperative' is gentler in tone than the imperative without *as*
cheere:	facial expression, hence general disposition, as in 'cheer up'
by youre fey!:	by your faith! A mild oath, possibly implying here 'as you promised' – the terms of the promise are explained in the next two lines
moot:	must
Lente:	the period including forty weekdays extending from Ash Wednesday to Easter-eve, observed as a time of prayer and fasting in commemoration of Jesus's fasting in the wilderness (see Luke 4:1–2)
termes:	technical stylistic constructions
colours:	rhetorical figures of speech
figures:	structural devices in literary composition (as in Modern English 'a figure of speech')
Heigh style:	ornate style
benignely:	gently
under youre yerde:	literally 'under your rod', hence 'under your authority'
obeisance:	obedience
hardily:	assuredly, at once
Padowe:	Padua
cheste:	coffin
Fraunceys Petrak, the lauriat poete:	Petrarch (1304–74) was the most famous Italian poet of the fourteenth century, writing in Latin and in Italian. His love poems to an unidentified woman, Laura, are among his most famous compositions. He was crowned poet laureate in Rome in 1341. His translation of Boccaccio's tale of Griselda was one of his last works

Lynyan:	Giovanni da Lignaco (1310?–83), a famous professor of canon law at Bologna. He also wrote on ethics, theology and astronomy. (The reference dates the composition of the tale to after 1383)
prohemye:	prologue
Pemond:	Piedmont
Saluces:	Saluzzo
Apennyn:	the Apennines
Lumbardye:	Lombardy
Vesulus:	Mount Viso (described as cold in line 58 because of its high altitude, 3,841 metres)
Poo:	the river Po
Emele-ward:	towards Emilia
Ferrare:	Ferrara
Venyse:	Venice
devyse:	describe
Me thynketh:	It seems to me
impertinent:	irrelevant
Save... mateere:	Except that he wishes to introduce his subject

---

The *Clerk's Tale:* the first part (lines 57–196)

A marquis lived in the fertile plain of Saluzzo. His name was Walter. He was handsome, young, carefree, well-bred and a bachelor. His people were worried because they feared that at his death the estate might pass to a stranger, and they urged him to marry. He was persuaded, stipulating only that his people must accept and honour whomsoever he chose to be his bride. They readily agreed and a day for the wedding was arranged. Preparations were at once begun for the grand feast.

NOTES AND GLOSSARY:

Incipit prima pars:	(Latin) The first part begins
highte:	is called
markys:	marquis. A nobleman usually holding lordship over a town or territory
whilom:	once upon a time
liges:	subjects
lasse and moore:	of low and of high rank (see 'Tags' pp. 47–8)
yoore:	for a long time
gentilleste:	most noble
fair:	handsome
gye:	govern
hym bityde:	happen to him
lust present:	immediate pleasure
othere cures leet he slyde:	he allowed other concerns to be set aside

nolde:	did not wish
for noght that may bifalle:	regardless of consequences
flokmeele:	in a group, crowd
loore:	learning
Or elles... Or elles:	either ... or
hardinesse:	courage
mowe:	may
hevynesse:	grief
pleyne:	make petition, complain
Al:	although
leste:	choose, wish
yok:	yoke (of marriage)
Ay:	constantly
fleeth the tyme... abyde:	time flies, it waits for no man
as stille as stoon:	as quietly as a stone
heeste:	command
chese:	choose
atte leeste:	at the least, at any rate
meeste:	greatest, most eminent
deeme:	judge
bisy drede:	nagging doubt, worry
slake:	cease
O, wo were us alyve!:	Oh how unhappy would we be!
Hir:	their
Ye wol... streyne me:	You, my own dear people, want to confine me to that which I never previously contemplated (that is, marriage)
seelde tyme:	seldom
Ther:	whereas
moot:	must
wit:	wisdom
streen:	strain, lineage
ybore:	born
hym bitake:	entrust to him
as hym leste:	as it pleases him
charge:	command
what:	whatever
dure:	last, endure
As:	as if
grucche:	grumble, complain
sith:	since
as evere moot I thryve:	a common mild oath, literally, 'So may I ever thrive'; hence 'upon my life' (see 'Tags', pp. 47–8)
but... manere:	unless you want to agree in this way

hertely:	enthusiastic
wight:	person
er:	before
hym leste:	pleased him, suited him
sikerly:	certainly
buxomly:	obediently
han:	have
purveye:	make provision
privee:	personal

Swich charge . . . leye: Gave [them] such responsibilities as he saw fit to entrust to them (literally, 'as it pleased him to put upon them')

Explicit prima pars: (Latin) The first part ends

The second part (lines 197–448)

In a village not far from Walter's palace there lived a peasant girl, Grisildis, with Janicula, her poor father. Walter had often observed her and determined that, if ever he should marry, it would be to Grisildis. She was of great virtue. Walter had gowns and jewellery prepared for his bride, and on the day appointed for the wedding rode out in a grand procession. Having obtained leave of the amazed Janicula, he offered himself in marriage to Grisildis demanding that, if she accepted, she must promise him her absolute obedience. She agreed and was arrayed in the fine clothes and jewels. Her renown for grace and virtue spread far and the people of Saluzzo, under her influence, lived in such concord that they judged that she had been sent from heaven. She soon gave birth to a daughter.

NOTES AND GLOSSARY:

Incipit secunda pars: (Latin) The second part begins

thilke:	that
Wher as:	where
shoop:	planned
throop:	village
delitable:	delightful
povre:	poor
hir:	their
herbergage:	dwellings

After . . . habundance: According to the abundance that the earth yielded

Which that:	who
holden:	held, considered
hye:	high

fair ynogh to sighte: very beautiful in appearance

Thanne:	then

oon the faireste:	one of the most beautiful
yfostred up:	brought up
likerous:	lustful
lust:	desire
yronne:	run, passed
tonne:	wine-cask
for she wolde vertu plese:	literally 'because she wanted to please virtue', hence 'because she was anxious to live virtuously'
noon ydel ese:	no idle laziness
rype:	mature
sad:	serious, steadfast
corage:	disposition, heart
spynnynge:	[for wool for] spinning
Wortes:	herbs
seeth:	boiled
for hir lyvynge:	to keep themselves fed (literally: 'for their living')
ful:	very
nothyng:	in no way
kepte ... on-lofte:	sustained her father's life
everich:	each, every
Ful ofte sithe:	Many a time
ye:	eye
paraventure:	by chance
fil:	happened
wantown lookyng of folye:	foolish and lustful gazing
sad wyse:	serious (steadfast) manner
chiere:	face
he wolde hym ofte avyse:	he frequently considered, deliberated
eek:	also
passynge:	surpassing
wight:	person
disposed:	planned
in privetee:	in privacy
vanytee:	foolishness
allas, the while!:	alas, the day!
bigile:	trick, deceive
hath doon make:	has had someone make
aornementes:	adornments
falle:	belong
undren:	a time of day which is not always clearly designated in Middle English. Usually 9 a.m. or 12 noon
ech in his degree:	each room according to its importance
maystow:	you can (*may + thou*)
deyntevous vitaille:	dainty food

as fer as last Ytaille: literally 'as far as last Italy', hence 'even in the most distant parts of Italy'

The whiche that: who

yprayed: invited

bachelrye: young knights/aspirants to knighthood

soun: sound, note

sondry: various

righte: direct

han holde: literally 'have held', hence 'took'

woot: knows

ful innocent: totally ignorant

shapen: planned, arranged

array: splendour

fayn: gladly

felawes: companions

fonde: endeavour

longeth: belongs, appertains

leyser: leisure

holde: makes her way

gan: the word in the past tense in Middle English often means 'began'; but it is also frequently used to give a more intense and dramatic tone to the verb and should, in such cases, be omitted in translation. It rests with the reader to decide which use of *gan* best suits a particular context

anon: at once

thresshfold: threshold

sad: serious

sobrely: gravely

cheere: facial expression, countenance

lette: delay

fette: fetched

vouche sauf: vouchsafe, permit

what so bityde: whatever may come of it

er: before

wende: depart

ybore: born

unto that purpos drawe: agree

cas: happening

astonyed: astonished

reed he wax: he grew red, blushed

abayst: abashed, embarrassed

unnethes: with difficulty

mo: more

ayeynes:	against, in opposition to
lust:	wish
governeth:	arrange (imperative form of the verb)
collacioun:	conference
reule hire:	regulate her conduct
audience:	earshot
tretys:	contract
wondred hem:	literally 'questioned themselves', hence 'queried, wondered'
tentifly:	attentively
outrely:	utterly
erst:	previously
woned:	accustomed
But shortly ... chace:	But briefly to relate the story
verray:	true
stonde:	be understood
axe:	ask
sith:	since
hastif wyse:	hasty manner
avyse:	think further about it
lust:	wishes
do:	make
smerte:	feel pain, sorrow
grucche it:	complain about it
ye:	yea, yes
undigne:	unworthy
beede:	offer
nyl:	(*ne + will*) will not
For to be deed:	Even though I were to die
looth:	loth, unwilling
geere:	clothes
dispoillen:	undress
han:	have
kembd:	combed
untressed:	unbraided, unplaited
corone:	crown
ydressed:	set
nowches:	brooches
Unnethe:	scarcely
for hire fairnesse:	because of her beauty
lette:	delayed
ladde:	led
in rudenesse:	roughly
cote:	cottage

norissed: raised
woxen: grown
ther: where
bore: born
trowed: believed
but dorste han swore: they would have dared swear
thewes: qualities
bountee: excellence
pees: peace
ynogh: enough, plenty
heelde: considered
seyn ful seelde: rarely seen
wit: intelligence, wisdom
Koude: understood
feet: feats, performance
hoomlinesse: domesticity
The commune . . . redresse: She could stand up for the general well-being of the people
hevynesse: grief
apese: ameliorate
ese: ease, comfort
anon: immediately
aton: together, in agreement
rype: mature
as men wende: as one believed; it was considered
Al had hire levere have born a knave child: Even though she would have preferred to have given birth to a baby boy
therfore: for it
al bifore: first
By liklihede . . . bareyne: In all probability since she is not sterile. The double negative, as in *nys nat* (= *ne* + *is nat*), is the usual form in Middle English
Explicit secunda pars: (Latin) The second part ends

The third part (lines 449–609)

A short while after the birth of the baby, Walter determined to test Grisildis's steadfastness in her promise to obey him without question. He told Grisildis that the people were unhappy at being governed by a woman of peasant origin, especially since the birth of her daughter, and that he therefore had no choice but remove the child. He instructed an officer of his household to go to Grisildis's room and seize the infant. Grisildis blessed her baby and begged the sergeant to bury the corpse so that animals and birds would not tear it to pieces. Walter told the sergeant the rest of the plan, namely that he must take the child carefully to Bologna to be looked after by Walter's sister, now married to the Earl of Panico. At no time during these events or after did Grisildis criticise her husband's actions.

NOTES AND GLOSSARY:

Incipit tercia pars: (Latin) The third part begins
Ther fil . . . mo: It came about, as on other occasions
souked: suckled
throwe: short while
sadnesse: steadfastness
assaye: test
yvele it sit: it ill befits
drede: fear, doubt
stierne: stern
cheere: facial expression
trowe: believe
For any wele ye moot youreselven knowe: In spite of any [subsequent] success, you must recognise this yourself
tweye: two
woot: know
lief: beloved
gentils: nobles
namely: especially, particularly
sith: since
recchelees: uncaring (of their wishes)
leste: wish
wityng: knowledge
in youre werkyng: in action
highte: promised
noght ameved: did not stir
spille: destroy
after: according to
Ther may . . . me: Nothing, so God save my soul, can please you which could displease me
leese: lose
save: except
ay: always
corage: heart, affections
drery: forbidding, ominous
a furlong wey or two: 'a short distance', but often referring to time, 'a couple of minutes or so'
prively: secretly
maner: kind of

sergeant:	the word had a wide range of meanings. In this context it probably means an officer of the household employed in enforcement of the law
privee man:	man who is a close personal attendant
Doon execucioun in:	carry out
dradde:	feared, respected
wiste:	knew
stalked hym:	stalked, came stealthily
stille:	quietly
moote:	must
foryeve:	forgive
thyng:	something
heestes:	commands
yfeyned:	avoided
men:	one (the word in the singular corresponds to French *on*, German *man*, as the third person singular impersonal pronoun)
moote nede:	must needs, must
hire:	their
lust:	wishes
hente:	seized
Despitously:	roughly
diffame:	ill-repute
wende:	believed
slawen:	slain
right tho:	instantly
nathelees:	nevertheless
syked:	sighed
to that the markys lyked:	to what pleased the marquis
atte:	at the
So as:	because, seeing that
gentil:	noble
barm:	bosom
blisse:	bless
sith:	since
thilke:	that
I hym bitake:	I deliver to him
shaltow:	shalt thou
norice:	nurse
reuthe:	pitiful sight
han:	have
but:	unless
torace:	tear it apart
cofre:	chest

lappe: wrapping of cloth

upon . . . swappe: on pain of death (literally, 'on pain of his head being cut off')

entente: plan

Panik: not positively identified, though there was a Panico some twenty miles south of Bologna

Bisekynge: beseeching

doon hire bisynesse: do all in her power

gentillesse: noble manners

for . . . bityde: whatever happens (probably a tag, see pp. 47−8, hence 'without fail')

But evere . . . kynde: Anything except unwaveringly steadfast and kind

wont: accustomed

every maner wyse: every [kind of] way

Noon . . . adversitee: No chance sign, in spite of any misfortune

doghter: daughter's

nempned: named

in . . . game: on any occasion (see 'Tags', pp. 47−8)

Explicit tercia pars: (Latin) The third part ends

The fourth part (lines 610−784)

Four years later Grisildis gave birth to a boy. When the child was two, Walter decided again to test Grisildis's patience by taking away the child as on the former occasion. He told Grisildis that the people objected to the prospect of being governed by a grandson of Janicula, and that he had to accede to their wishes. Grisildis replied that her desire was to be obedient to Walter's will. The sergeant removed the child, and the people, on hearing the rumour that Walter had murdered both children on account of Grisildis's low birth, grew to hate him. When the daughter was twelve, Walter contrived that letters should be sent as if from the Pope authorising him to divorce and remarry. He then asked the Earl of Panico (his sister's husband) to proclaim that the young girl (his own daughter) was to marry him, and she, with her seven-year-old brother, set out in grand procession towards Saluzzo.

NOTES AND GLOSSARY:

Sequitur pars quarta: (Latin) The fourth part follows

knave: boy

herye: praise

Departed: parted

caughte yet another lest: literally, 'had yet another desire', hence, 'wished yet again'

tempte: test

yet ofter:	even further
assay:	trial
mesure:	moderation
sikly berth:	bear ill, disapprove of
namely:	especially
murmur:	complaint
corage:	heart, spirit
smerte:	sharply
ny:	nearly
agon:	gone, dead
out of drede:	without doubt, indeed
sentence:	opinion
Though . . . audience:	Even though they do not openly state their views within my hearing
wolde:	would, wish to
disposed outrely:	fully determined
servede:	treated
Out . . . outreye:	Not be beside yourself [or, out of your mind] with grief
I wol . . . certayn:	I want nothing, and indeed shall not wish for anything
Naught greveth me:	Nothing distresses me
I have . . . tweyne:	I have had nothing from my two children
axeth no reed at me:	do not ask for my opinion
plesaunce:	pleasure, happiness
wiste I:	if I knew
do yow ese:	make you content, please you
say:	saw
array:	condition, situation
if . . . devyse:	if one can imagine worse
hent:	seized
evere in oon:	constantly
grave:	bury
as . . . roghte:	as if he did not care at all
This markys wondred, evere lenger the moore:	The more the time passed, the more the marquis was perpetually amazed. Literally, 'the longer, the greater'; *the* in this construction means 'thereby'. (Compare Modern English constructions, such as 'the sooner the better')
Upon:	about, concerning
in every wyse:	in all respects
fayn:	willingly
sturdy:	cruel
stynte:	stop

right as:	just as if
slake:	desist
He waiteth if...:	He waits [to see] whether ...
ay oon:	literally, 'always one', hence 'constant'
And ay...age:	And all the time the older she became
penyble:	inured to pain
that of hem two...wyl:	literally, 'that between the two of them there was only one will', that is, 'that they were always of one mind'
al fil:	everything turned out
She shewed...wolde:	She well illustrated that a wife should in fact desire nothing for herself, on account of any worldly discomfort, but only what her husband wished
sclaundre:	scandal
For:	because
ere:	ear
diffame:	ill-repute
for ernest ne for game:	literally, 'neither for serious or lighthearted [reason].' A tag (see pp. 47–8) meaning 'on no account'
stente:	cease
entente:	purpose
wyse:	manner
bulles:	Papal bulls, documents bearing the official seal
reste:	peace
lete:	forsake
rude:	poor, simple
wo:	unhappy
ylike sad for everemo:	steadfast as ever
As to...suffisance:	For her true worldly contentment
tho:	literally 'then', hence 'previously'
outrely:	absolutely
shapynge:	making
Explicit quarta pars:	(Latin) The fourth part ends

The fifth part (lines 785–938)

Walter publicly announced to Grisildis that he was compelled to yield to the desire of his people to marry someone of rank, and that the Pope had permitted him to divorce. Grisildis replied that she was grateful for the years of a marriage of which she was unworthy, and that she would go back to Janicula's house. She returned all her possessions to Walter, but begged him to allow her to keep a smock so that she did not have to walk naked before the people. Her request was granted and she went home dry-eyed, followed by the grief-stricken crowd. She lived humbly with her father, and never complained about Walter's harsh treatment.

NOTES AND GLOSSARY:

Sequitur pars quinta: (Latin) The fifth part follows

after:	in keeping with
usage:	customary behaviour
To . . . corage:	To the extreme testing of her nature
loore:	knowledge
boistously:	roughly, bluntly
sentence:	opinion, judgement
lynage:	lineage, descent
avyse:	consider
sondry wyse:	various ways, several respects
constreyneth:	(third person plural of verb) force, compel
slake:	abate, assuage
that . . . undertake:	literally 'that I dare warrant', hence 'certainly', 'indeed'
is . . . weye:	is [already] on her way here
voyde:	quit, depart from
anon:	immediately
dowere:	dowry
Retourneth:	(imperative plural of verb: plural is used to agree with the possessive pronoun *youre*, see '"Thou" and "ye"', pp. 44–6) return!
With . . . aventure:	I advise you to endure the blows of fortune or chance with quiet courage
woot, and wiste:	know and knew
it is no nay:	there is no denying it
heeld:	considered
digne:	worthy
chamberere:	chambermaid
And also . . . glaade:	So in his wisdom may he bring my soul to happiness
dure:	endure, last
benignitee:	kindness
Foryelde:	reward
it is no drede:	certainly
God shilde:	God forbid
make:	mate
wele:	happiness
wont:	accustomed
whilom:	formerly
nothyng faire:	literally 'not at all beautiful', hence 'plain'

sooth is seyd:	it is truly said
algate:	always
in effect:	actually
Love . . . newe:	New love has not had time to grow stale (literally, 'love is not old when it is new')
To . . . cas:	Even if I were to die through this mischance
dide me streepe:	commanded me to be stripped
weede:	clothes
Inwith:	within
dar I saufly sayn:	certainly (literally, 'I dare safely say')
smoklees:	without a smock
lyk a worm:	proverbial expression, 'as naked as a worm', hence 'stark naked'
gerdon:	reward, recompense
As voucheth sauf:	vouchsafe, grant
meede:	reward
wrye:	conceal
here:	her
wel unnethes:	with great difficulty
routhe:	compassion
is she fare:	she made her way
Shoop . . . creature:	Made him a living creature
in suspect:	suspicious, doubtful
demed:	judged
corage:	sexual desires
disparage:	disparagement, disgrace
t'alighte:	to step down
voyden:	send away
Agayns:	towards
as it myghte be:	as best as possible
fele:	many
flour:	flower
as by:	to judge by
goost:	spirit
tendre mouth:	fastidiousness over food
herte delicaat:	literally 'dainty heart' or 'delicate heart', hence something like 'ultra-refined sensibility'
semblant:	appearance
whan hem list:	literally 'when it pleases them', hence 'from time to time'
endite:	write, relate
lite:	little
acquite:	equal
but . . . newe:	unless things have changed recently

The sixth part (lines 939–1218)
and *Lenvoy de Chaucer*

The Earl of Panico arrived at Saluzzo, bringing the (supposed) new marchioness. Walter sent for Grisildis and commanded her to make ready the palace for the new bride. Grisildis worked hard to prepare for the wedding feast. She told Walter how much she admired the beauty of the young woman; but begged him to treat her with tenderness because her gentle nurturing would have made her less resilient than a peasant girl. Walter was at last convinced and explained that all the hardships had been tests of her steadfastness. Grisildis, overwhelmed with joy, was re-instated as marchioness and the feast continued in an atmosphere of supreme happiness. Walter and Grisildis lived happily for the rest of their lives, and their son eventually succeeded his father.

The Clerk explained that the story was not to be taken literally, but that it was a moral allegory about the testing of man by God. He confessed that women like Grisildis would be difficult to find and (playfully) praised the attitudes of the Wife of Bath. (The scribe attributes part of this passage to Chaucer rather than the Clerk. But it is quite in keeping with the Clerk's ironic tone.) Harry Bailly praised the Clerk for his tale.

NOTES AND GLOSSARY:

to moore and lesse: probably, 'to everyone', 'universally', (see 'Tags',
pp. 47 – 8)

eres:	ears
alle and some:	one and all
kouth:	known
ye:	eye
shoop:	planned
sely:	innocent
corage:	heart
heste:	command
hire sette:	set herself down
in his degree:	in accordance with his rank
Have his estaat:	Should be given proper status
suffisaunt:	adequate, sufficiently capable
ordinaunce:	order
yvel biseye:	ill-looking
devoir:	duty
at the leeste weye:	in any case
goost:	spirit
stente:	cease
dighte:	prepare

chambereres:	chambermaids
undren:	9 a.m. or 12 noon
governaunce:	management
unsad:	fickle
fane:	weather-cock
rumbul:	rumour
clappyng:	chatter
jane:	a Genoese coin worth a halfpenny. Hence proverbially something of little value: *deere ynogh a jane*, 'not worth a halfpenny'
doom:	judgement

youre constance yvele preeveth: your constancy proves to be unreliable

leeveth:	believes
dresse:	address my attention
abayst:	abashed, disconcerted
torent:	torn
konnyngly:	wisely
koude:	knew

koude hir prys amende: could improve upon her estimation

wende:	decided
in good fey:	in truth faith, indeed
mo:	others

she is fostred in hire norissynge: she has been brought up

dresse:	set in a state (of mind), prepare

agast ne yvele apayed: frightened or ill-pleased

assayed:	tested

took of it no keep: did not notice it

ferde:	existed

mazednesse abreyde: awoke from her amazement

disposed:	planned
aswowne:	in a swoon
Grauntmercy:	(from French *grand* + *merci*) many thanks

God thanke it yow: May God reward you

'Now . . . heere': 'Now I do not care if I die on this very spot', or '. . . at this very moment'

No fors of deeth: Death does not matter

pace:	sets forth, parts

Hath doon yow kept: Have had you preserved. The structure singular verb ('hath') + double subject ('God . . . And youre benyngne fader') was acceptable in Middle English. We would use 'have'

stounde:	moment
swapte:	fell
sadly:	steadfastly, firmly

sleighte: skill

arace: remove

Unnethe: scarcely, with difficulty

abaysed: disconcerted

And every . . . maketh: And everyone [tried to] make her happy, and honoured her

caught agayn hir contenaunce: recovered her composure

deyntee: delight

yfeere: together

say: saw

as hire oghte: as was befitting for her

dispende: pass

welkne: sky

solempne: splendid

costage: expense

Al: although

it is no nay: there is no denying it

this auctour: this author (Petrarch)

inportable, though they wolde: intolerable even if they desired to do so

heigh stile: the phrase appears also in lines 18 and 41. It means 'ornate' or 'rhetorically splendid'. (It is probable that Chaucer's manuscript of Petrarch's letter to Boccaccio (see p. 36) wrongly had the reading *stylo alto* (high style) for the correct *stylo alio* (another style). Boccaccio had written in Italian and Petrarch tells him in the letter that for his version of the story he has decided to use 'another style' – that is, Latin)

in gree: with a good will

For greet . . . wroghte: For it is very reasonable that he should test that which he created

But he ne tempteth . . . drede: the reference is to the Epistle of James, 1:13: 'Let no man say when he is tempted, I am tempted of God; for God cannot be tempted with evil, neither tempteth he any man,' (*Authorised Version of the Bible*). The Clerk is distinguishing between the two Middle English meanings of 'tempt' ((i) 'test' and (ii) 'persuade to do evil') by contrasting *tempteth* with *preeveth* in the next line. Thus the lines mean: 'But – as St James remarks, if you read his epistle – God does not persuade mankind, whom he redeemed, to sin; [though] certainly he constantly tests people'

suffreth: permits

freletee:	frailty
suffraunce:	patience
o:	one
swiche assayes:	such tests
alayes:	alloys
at ye:	to the eye
breste:	break
plye:	bend

for the Wyves love of Bathe: for love of the Wife of Bath. See discussion on p. 39

secte: sect. The Clerk uses the word ironically, as if the Wife of Bath's hedonistic beliefs were a kind of religion with its own followers. (The Middle English *secte* could, however, mean 'sex': in that case the phrase would mean 'the Wife of Bath . . . and all other women')

scathe:	a pity
Seyn yow a song:	Recite a poem to you
to glade yow:	to cheer you up
wene:	believe

Lenvoy de Chaucer: Chaucer's epilogue. (The epilogue continues in the same satirical vein as the Clerk has shown in the preceding stanza, and it thus seems that the heading *Lenvoy de Chaucer* may be an unnecessary scribal addition.) The six-line stanza form is, however, different from the rhyme-royal (a seven-line stanza) of the rest of the poem

atones:	at once, simultaneously
hardy:	rash
in trust to fynde:	expecting to find
naille:	nail, fasten
diligence:	effort. The word evidently means, in this context, 'spend his energy'
Chichevache:	The Lean Cow. A proverbial medieval monster which fed on patient wives – the shortage of whom led to the monster's leanness
swelwe:	swallow
entraille:	entrails, stomach
Ekko:	Echo. A reference to the mountain nymph, Echo, in Greek mythology. There are several stories about her, variously accounting for her disembodied voice and for her repeating other speakers' last words. The implication here is that women should always have the final word

countretaille: reply, answer back. (When a debt was recorded on a tally-stick, a counter-tally-stick – a duplicate – was sometimes kept by the other party. Thus, in the present context, the word may mean 'pay back' in an aggressive sense)

bidaffed: fooled

governaille: mastery

Emprenteth: imprint (imperative form of the verb)

For commune . . . availle: Since it may be of assistance to the general good

archewyves: dominating wives

camaille: camel

And sklendre . . . Ynde: And you slim wives, weak though you would be in battle, be as fierce as the tiger of far-away India

Ay: constantly, incessantly

clappeth as a mille: chatter like a mill, nag (a proverbial phrase in Middle English)

consaille: advise

maille: chain-mail

aventaille: hinged section of a helmet

couche as doth a quaille: cower like a [hunted] quail

ther: when

visage: face

fre: liberal, generous

dispence: spending

ay do thy travaille: constantly strive

of chiere: cheerful

as light as leef on lynde: as light as the leaf on a lime tree (proverbial)

wrynge: wring [his hands in despair]

Me were levere: I had rather

This is . . . wille: literally, 'This is a noble story for the occasion, regarding my intention, if you knew my wish'. The sense is clear, though the structure is elliptical. *For the nones* ('for that once') sometimes means 'for the occasion', but is often a tag used as an intensifier to mean 'indeed, certainly' (see 'Tags', pp. 47–8). The whole passage could be translated, 'If you knew my wish you would agree that this is indeed an excellent story to further my plan'. The Host's confessedly forlorn hope is to persuade his wife to be as obedient as Grisildis

But . . . stille: But what cannot be is best left alone (proverbial). The Host means that, as his wife is unlikely to change, there is no point in stirring up trouble

Part 3

Commentary

Sources and analogues: the 'Patient Wife' motif

We know that Chaucer used Petrarch's Latin version of the story and also a close translation of Petrarch in French. These, then, are the immediate sources of the *Clerk's Tale*. The ultimate source of the story of the patient wife is probably an oral folk tale. The tale appears in a number of versions in medieval Europe, two of which in particular bear close resemblances to the *Clerk's Tale*. It is instructive to see how the plot is adapted by its various authors in order to bring out the particular aspects of the characters and of the tale which they judge to be important. (We do not know, incidentally, whether Chaucer was acquainted with the story other than through the Petrarch version.)

1. *Lai le Freisne*

The tale is told by Marie de France in the twelfth century in Norman-French. A fourteenth-century translation of the poem also exists in English (entitled *Lai le Freine*).

Two knights are close friends. The wife of one produces twin boys, and the jealous wife of the other maliciously says that the woman must have made love to two men. Shortly afterwards the jealous wife gives birth to twin girls. In order to avoid the effect of her own ridiculous scandal-mongering she has a servant take one baby and carry it away by night. Wrapping it in a rich cloth, the servant-girl leaves the baby in the hollow of an ash tree (compare Modern French *frêne* = ash) near a convent. In addition to the cloth, the baby possesses a gold ring. The nuns rear the child and she grows into a beautiful young woman. She is wooed by a rich and powerful knight, Sir Guroun, who has heard good reports of her. He persuades her to steal away from the convent and they live for a long time in his castle as man and wife. The people of the estate love her, but after a while some of Sir Guroun's retainers request him to wed the daughter of a man of rank so that his heir will be high-born rather than the offspring of a woman whose origins are obscure. Guroun agrees and the wedding is arranged. Le Freisne, though broken-hearted, works harder than any of the servants in preparing the feast. She notices that the bed covers are poor and she spreads out the fine cloth in which she had been wrapped when abandoned. The mother of the new bride recognises the cloth, is also shown the gold ring, and confesses her guilty secret. Le Freisne is, after all, married to Sir Guroun.

2. *Fair Annie*

A Scottish ballad, probably of medieval origin, has many similarities. There are a number of versions but the main story-line is as follows: Annie is stolen away from her home by a lord from over the sea. She bears him seven (illegitimate) sons. The lord (in some versions because of the lure of a rich dowry) decides to marry a foreign lady. He commands Annie to prepare a welcome for the new bride. Though distressed, she does so, but on the wedding night the lady hears Annie weeping. She goes to her, discovers that they are sisters and sails home leaving Annie with some of her treasure-ships so that she may have a dowry and (not before time) marry her lord.

Many of the main elements of these stories are those emphasised also in the *Clerk's Tale*: the cruel humiliation of the heroine when rejected; the added poignancy when she does her utmost to make a fitting welcome for the new bride who will displace her; the recognition scene where it is found that the new bride is a close relation of the heroine. But there are differences of emphasis, some of which will become clearer as we trace the story a little further.

3. Boccaccio: the *Decameron*

Chaucer acknowledges that he derived his story from Petrarch; Petrarch acknowledges that he derived his from Boccaccio. Although Chaucer used several of Boccaccio's works as a basis for his own poems, he had almost certainly not read the *Decameron*, which contains the Griselda tale.

Our chief purpose here is to focus on the *Clerk's Tale*, but it is necessary to be aware of some of the 'unknowns' as we look at the development of the story under various hands. We do not know, for example, whether Chaucer knew the story (perhaps in oral form) other than via Petrarch. Nor do we know in what form Boccaccio heard the tale. Indeed, on this last point, there has been much discussion, including the theory that there is an underlying influence of folk tales of the Cupid and Psyche type, in which a supernatural lover sets a taboo requirement on his (or her) mortal mate, just as Walter demands the unquestioning obedience of Grisildis. Given this reservation, then, that in speaking of Boccaccio's treatment of a folk tale, we are dealing with likelihoods, not proven facts, it is nevertheless a convenient way of focusing our minds on the elements of the story to make some comparisons. We can reasonably assume that Boccaccio based his tale on a story of the *le Freisne* and *Fair Annie* type. Those tales concentrate on a few basic episodes:

1. A lord keeps as his mistress a girl of obscure origin.
2. For motives of financial or social gain, he decides to marry someone else. (Guroun, in *le Freisne* agrees, though reluctantly, to the demands of some of his knights; in *Fair Annie*, the lord himself promotes the plan to marry a rich woman.)
3. The displaced mistress works hard to prepare the food, or the house, for the new bride. She is heart-broken but conceals her grief.
4. The discovery is made that the bride and the mistress are sisters.
5. The lord marries the mistress.

It matters little in the present discussion whether Boccaccio invented the further developments of this plot or found them elsewhere. What does matter is that the form of his story contains elements which enable a longer, more thought-provoking version to be told. The increased duration of time (twelve years) and the greater number of cruelties visited upon Griselda make her treatment utterly shocking:

1. Griselda is the wife, not mistress, of Gualtieri, making her rejection even more harsh.
2. Her daughter is taken away, evidently to be murdered.
3. Two years later, the same fate befalls her son.
4. Ten years later, she is told that Gualtieri is divorcing her and she is sent home in peasant dress.
5. She is summoned back to prepare the palace for a new bride, and told that she will afterwards be sent back again to her father's cottage.

At the end of all this, she learns that Gualtieri had simply wished to test her patience and had pretended to murder the children, and so on, just to see whether she would reject his authority.

Boccaccio's story is a tale-within-a-tale. Some noble ladies and gentlemen flee from Florence to avoid the plague, and while away the time by telling stories and discussing them. Dioneo tells this, the final story. It is, he says, about the ridiculous brutality of a marquis: 'Even though good eventually came of his actions, no one should imitate him; he did not deserve the happy outcome of his cruel tests.' Dioneo then draws a general moral from his story: 'Divine souls are sometimes rained down from heaven into poor houses, while in royal palaces are born those who are better fitted to herd swine than to rule over men.'

We see, then, that the story is becoming more abstract, is asking us not only to feel pity for the heroine and indignation at the behaviour of her lover, but to speculate further about the nature of nobility: is it a matter of one's birth or of one's actions? Le Freisne and Annie behave nobly – but then they *are* nobly-born even if they do not know it. Because Griselda is indeed a peasant by birth and yet behaves with such serene dignity we are in a position to recognise that social rank is an irrelevance where true nobility of character is concerned.

---

4. Petrarch *Epistolae Seniles* (Book 17, Letter 3)

Petrarch's translation into Latin prose of Boccaccio's Italian version (also in prose) was made almost at the end of his life. He dedicated his translation to Boccaccio and enclosed with it a long letter discussing the story. His story, being in Latin, was available to an international readership (Latin being the universally accepted language of the cultured in the Middle Ages), though it simultaneously limited the readership to those who were highly educated.

The hint at abstracting, at considering the question of true nobility, which we had noticed in Dioneo's account of the tale, is taken a stage further in Petrarch by presenting the story as a religious allegory in a way that would have no doubt pleased its scholarly readers. 'My object,' writes Petrarch in his covering letter to Boccaccio, 'in thus re-writing your tale was not to induce the women of our time to imitate the patience of this wife, which seems to me almost beyond imitation, but to lead my readers to emulate the example of feminine constancy, and to submit themselves to God with the same courage as did this woman to her husband.'* He goes on in the letter to recount the effect of his story on two friends: one, from Padua, is so overcome with grief at its sadness that he cannot finish reading it, the other, from Verona, remains dry-eyed because he believes that the fortitude of Griselda is so extreme as to be incredible.† Yet, says Petrarch, history shows us that there have been men and women whose courage in adversity has been as remarkable.

---

5. The *Clerk's Tale*

(a) The allegorical detail

Petrarch develops the theme of the suffering of the innocent by comparing the innate nobility of Griselda with that of Christ. She was born in a peasant's hovel but, says Petrarch, we may recall that once upon

---

* Translated by J.H. Robinson, *Petrarch*, G.P. Putnam's Sons, New York and London, 1898, p. 194.
† For an interesting discussion of Petrarch's letter see Anne Middleton, 'The Clerk and his tale: some literary contexts', *Studies in the Age of Chaucer*, Vol.2, University of Oklahoma, 1980, pp. 121–50.

a time the grace of God descended into a poor dwelling. Chaucer further emphasises such allegorical hints. For Petrarch's 'poor dwelling' he substitutes the more specific biblical reference 'litel oxes stalle' (line 207). Perhaps, too, the reaction of men to Christ – now popular, now rejected – is hinted at in Chaucer's addition to Petrarch's story in lines 995–1001. In a more general way Griselda's ready submission to suffering brings to our minds Christ's words in the Garden of Gethsemane, 'Nevertheless not my will, but thine, be done'.

Petrarch had added an allusion to the patient suffering of Job which God permitted as a test of his constancy. Chaucer retains this quotation (lines 871–2) but he adds another (lines 902–3) and in line 932 he makes specific reference to the Book of Job. Job was proverbially the ultimate example of the patient suffering of an innocent man. God permitted Satan to inflict upon Job all kinds of suffering because he was convinced that Job would never renounce him. Job withstands the tests, and when he questions the suffering of the innocent, God appears to him and explains that it is not for man to question his supreme wisdom.

(b) The realistic detail

At the same time, Chaucer (or the Clerk) adds to the realism of Petrarch's account. Some of these additions are too minor to note here. But from the longer passages we may infer a subtle change of emphasis.

Lines	Additions
260–94:	many details of the grand procession
460–2:	the Clerk's remonstration against Walter's cruelty
554–67:	Grisildis's farewell to her baby daughter
621–3:	a further remonstration (compare lines 460–2 above)
811–12:	Walter advises Grisildis to endure the strokes of fortune
837–40:	Grisildis swears that she could never remarry
851–61:	Grisildis recalls to Walter his loving tenderness on their wedding day. She laments that love grows cold and promises that she will never regret giving her love to Walter
881–2:	Grisildis tells Walter that he should bear in mind that she was his wife and not humiliate her too shamefully
932–8:	the Clerk mentions the patience of Job and goes on to say that though clerks often praise the humble steadfastness of men, that of women is even greater
990–1:	the people consider that the children of the new marriage will be more beautiful than those of Grisildis, because of the new bride's aristocratic origins
995–1005:	the lament over the fickleness of public opinion

Lines	Additions
1079–1106:	a very greatly expanded version of the dénouement scene. (In Petrarch we hear only that Griselda fainted from a mixture of joy and sorrow. The ladies dressed her again in her fine clothes. Everyone was overjoyed.) All details about the embracing of her children, and so on, are the Clerk's addition

From the above table, it is clear that the Clerk is at pains to stress the emotional agonies of Grisildis. She becomes less passively compliant, and indeed several times gently rebukes Walter for his cruelty. Indignation against Walter is voiced both in these rebukes and by the Clerk himself.

(c) The tension between realism and allegory

In these ways, the too-good-to-be-true Griselda becomes humanised, and it is easier to sympathise with her. It brings us back to the reaction which Petrarch encountered in his friends from Padua and Verona, mentioned above. On the other hand it may be objected that the Clerk's emphasis on Walter's harshness makes it potentially more difficult for us to accept an allegorical interpretation of the story in which Grisildis represents the patient soul and Walter represents God who allows us to be scourged with the whip of adversity (lines 1156–8). The more realistic the story becomes, the more we may be outraged at the tyrant, Walter. This tension between representational and literal is one that readers must work out for themselves. Certainly, the Host and the Merchant (who tells the next tale) take the story on the literal level in spite of the Clerk's recommendation to see the tale as allegory: both pilgrims are put in mind of their own wives and their shrewishness. But, as we shall see in the next section, even the Clerk tells his tale with more than one aim in mind.

(d) A tale-within-a-tale

In the *General Prologue to the Canterbury Tales* Chaucer introduces the twenty-nine pilgrims who intend to travel from the Tabard Inn in London to the shrine of St Thomas Becket in Canterbury Cathedral. It is decided by Harry Bailly, landlord of the Tabard Inn, that each pilgrim shall tell four stories – two on the way to Canterbury, two more on the return journey. This vast scheme was never completed. What we have is a series of nine fragments or groups of tales, though the order of these fragments is not consistent in the various manuscript collections. The third, fourth and fifth fragments in the generally accepted order of modern editions do, however, appear to have been intended as a consistent sequence by Chaucer: there is a natural inter-relationship between the seven tales which make up those fragments. The seven are the Tales (with their Prologues) told by the Wife of Bath, the Friar, the Summoner, the Clerk, the Merchant, the Squire and the Franklin. The Prologues are the connecting links between tales where the pilgrims comment on the tale that has just ended and where Harry Bailly calls upon the next story-teller. In these links there is often a development of the character-sketches we had seen in the *General Prologue*, and we become increasingly aware of rivalries and antipathies between some of the pilgrims. Indeed, the tales told by some pilgrims are a projection of their own personalities and an opportunity to mock other pilgrims against whom they feel personal animosity.

G.L. Kittredge* suggests persuasively that, in four tales of this seven-tale sequence, Chaucer presents us with a debate on the subject of marriage. These are the *Wife of Bath's Tale*, the *Clerk's Tale*, the *Merchant's Tale* and the *Franklin's Tale*, and the (albeit interrupted) sequence is sometimes known as the 'Marriage Group'. The five-times-married Wife of Bath at the end of her tale prays that men who will not be ruled by their wives may die prematurely. In her outrageous Prologue, she makes disparaging comments on clerks who preach against sexual licence. Her fifth husband was finally forced to obey her authority which he had challenged by reading aloud stories of wicked wives. He was an Oxford clerk.

Our Clerk does not immediately react to these taunts, but his shy manner (see line 2 of the *Prologue to the Clerk's Tale*) conceals the devastating irony of which he is capable. He is careful to point out that his tale is told by a clerk (lines 31–2) and that wise people regard co-operation in marriage as the recipe for happiness (lines 113–14). At the end of his story he, like Petrarch before him, explains that he has not intended the moral of his story to be taken literally (lines 1142–7) and prays (in a sly leg-pull) that God will maintain the Wife of Bath and others whose views conform to hers. He continues (lines 1183–1212) in tongue-in-cheek praise of domineering wives. Harry Bailly is reminded of his wife and the Merchant follows with a lament over his own disastrous marriage before relating his black comedy on marriage.

In this way an extra dimension of critical response is called for as we read the *Clerk's Tale*. It is complete in itself and yet at the same time interconnected with the whole dialectic on marriage. It is a reply to the heretical views of the Wife of Bath while being, on the personal level, the Clerk's subtle revenge for her mockery of clerks. To read the *Clerk's Tale* without regard to the portraits of the Clerk and Wife of Bath in the *General Prologue*, and also to the *Prologue to the Wife of*

* See his 'Chaucer's Discussion of Marriage', *Modern Philology*, Vol. 9, 1911–12, pp. 435–67. See Part 5, Suggestions for further reading, for references to this article.

Bath's Tale, is to read in isolation a story whose full meaning can be appreciated only by setting the tale in this wider context.

Characterisation

The question of characterisation has been discussed on pp. 33–40, where the presentation of the protagonists of the story by Boccaccio, Petrarch and Chaucer was compared. It may be of help, however, to summarise and develop the main points raised.

The crux of the problem of interpreting the story of Grisildis is indicated by Petrarch, when he recounts that his friend from Padua is overcome with grief on hearing about her sufferings, while the friend from Verona finds the story unmoving because incredible. The third approach to the story (Petrarch's own) is that it is a model to represent the proper reaction of man to the tests put upon him by God. Yet Petrarch himself is not willing to let his story go simply as allegory, but adds that history has shown us that there have been men and women as patient as Grisildis.

The same tension, the same dilemma of interpretation, is inherent in the *Clerk's Tale*. In spite of the Clerk's assurances that the story is a moral allegory, Harry Bailly and, immediately after, the Merchant, take the story on a literal level and contrast Grisildis with their own shrewish wives. Furthermore, as we have seen in the earlier discussions, the Clerk himself criticises Walter's treatment of Grisildis, and he allows her some moments of remonstration which he did not find in Petrarch's version (see pp. 37–8).

On the literal plane, Walter is too petty, too cruel in extending his test of a demonstrably perfect and obedient woman. Yet his obsession gives him pain, too, as noted in the discussion of *thou* and *ye* (pp. 44–6). It is as if we see a man driven by doubt in spite of all evidence to the contrary, and he is saved from our dismissal as an inhuman tyrant by the knowledge that his tormenting of Grisildis is also self-tormenting. The touches of humanity in Chaucer's version make us hesitate before denouncing him (as Dioneo denounced Gualtieri) as a man fit only to herd swine (see p. 35).

Of course this does not decrease the unfairness of the treatment Grisildis receives even if it mitigates the harshness of our judgement of Walter. The Clerk's simple language, the quiet dignity of his recounting of his story is perfectly suited to the dignity of its chief character and her sombre story. She is at once actively tender and caring in her relationship with her father and in her solicitude for her children, and passively receptive like the great biblical examples of undefiled spiritual perfection, Rebecca and Mary. In the stanza composed of lines 288–94 these connotations come together: the pitcher at the well reminds us of that scene (Genesis 24) when Rebecca's standing by the well with her pitcher is the prelude to her marriage with Isaac; the 'oxes stall' is reminiscent of Mary in the stable with the infant Jesus, and perhaps the quiet acceptance of the command, as she falls to her knees, is an oblique reference to the Annunciation. Elsewhere in these Notes are mentioned the specific references to Job, the great medieval exemplar of patient suffering, and to Christ's acceptance of suffering (see p. 37) and the turning of the people against him (see p. 37).

That Grisildis is not mechanically obedient, but inwardly in emotional agony is emphasised throughout, and most notably in the Clerk's additions to Petrarch's account in the scene when she is reunited with her children in lines 1079–1106 (see p. 38).

Homeliness of touch is seen in the stuttering terrors of Janicula when Walter speaks to him early in the poem, and in the revelation that he had always doubted the constancy of Walter's love, towards the end.

When Jesus explains the allegorical meaning of one of his parables to his disciples (Luke 8: 10), he tells them that some people are allowed to see the mysteries of the kingdom of God, but that God speaks to others in parables, 'that seeing they might not see, and hearing they might not understand'. The simple moral that Harry Bailly deduces from the story, 'I just wish my wife could hear that story', no doubt was different from that deduced by the scholarly Poor Parson. Yet allegory is not a matter of literal versus allegorical. Even if the scholarly theologians in the company could see the representative functions of Walter (God) and Grisildis (the pure soul who unflinchingly accepts God's tests), they also, no doubt, could see the literal and moving account of the peasant girl who would not swerve from her promise, and perhaps recall, as Petrarch recalled, that history proves that such patience is not without precedent.

Medieval clerks

The word 'clerk' had a wide range of meanings in the Middle Ages. It indicated a man of learning and was specifically used to denote a priest, a university student or graduate, or an official in charge of records or accounts in local or central government.

There were only two universities in England in Chaucer's day: Oxford (founded around 1167) and Cambridge (founded around 1209). They were, of course, very much smaller than they are today, though new colleges were erected at both universities during Chaucer's lifetime.

Many students of theology hoped to obtain ecclesiastical appointments, but the number of posts was limited and those who could afford to continue their studies did so, hoping that they would eventually be offered a church living (see *General Prologue*, line 291).

Clearly, Chaucer's Clerk had set his heart on priestly employment and was not attracted to the secular posts for which his intellectual attainments would have made him a strong candidate. To him 'worldly' office, even though well rewarded financially, would have necessitated an unacceptable curtailing of his opportunities for study (see *General Prologue*, lines 292–6, quoted on pp. 8–9).

Thus, with no income of his own, he relied on family financial support to meet his university fees and also his day-to-day expenses of food and clothing. Of both these commodities he had a meagre supply (see *General Prologue*, lines 287–90). Chaucer says that the Clerk was funded by his 'friends': that word could carry the Modern English meaning, but it could also mean 'relations' and, given the context, the latter meaning is more likely in this instance. The situation was a common one at the time. The Oxford Clerk, Nicholas, in Chaucer's *Miller's Tale*, was financed by 'friends', and Chaucer's great contemporary poet William Langland, author of *Piers Plowman*, tells us that his educational expenses were met by his father and his 'friends'.

Middle English

1. Language

The principal stages in the development of the English language are known as Old English (or Anglo-Saxon), Middle English (dating from about 1150 to 1500) and Modern English.

Old English dates from around AD449, when Teutonic tribes first began to settle in Britain. The indigenous people had been Celtic-speaking, using a tongue of which Modern Welsh is a descendant. Probably, as England had been a Roman province, Latin, too, was widely understood and spoken.

Old English was highly inflected – in many respects similar to Modern German – and was more or less consistent in form over the areas in which it was spoken, even though there were regional dialectal variations. A fine, sophisticated corpus of Old English literature has survived, of which the most famous work is the long epic poem *Beowulf*.

Foreign invasion dramatically changed the course of English after the Norman Conquest of 1066. Administration of the country fell to French speakers, many of whom did not understand English and the native tongue was inevitably affected: though French grammatical forms and idioms influenced English only a little, there were extensive borrowings from French vocabulary, and, most radically, the complex Old English inflectional endings (indicating cases and tenses) were much simplified. In Chaucer, for example, virtually all noun plurals end with the letter -s (as in Modern English), whereas in Old English there had been a complex system of plural indicators.

Until the end of the fourteenth century, the ability to speak French was necessary for the middle and upper classes (or at least considered socially desirable), and it was the language of administration and the law. Linguistic changes and influences varied in different geographical regions, and distinct dialects developed. So different could they be that at the end of *Troilus and Criseyde* Chaucer begs scribes who make copies of the poem to follow exactly what he has written because 'there are so many dialects in England that a scribe unused to my [London] dialect may mis-transcribe the poem, and thus ruin the metre'.

For a number of reasons (such as the importance of the court and central administration, of the prosperity which the port brought with its trade, and the proximity of the two universities) the London dialect became dominant, and, by the late fifteenth century, it was the standard for the written language.

The settling down of the language after these upheavals (coupled with the advent of printing which stabilised the written form in the second half of the fifteenth century) marks the end of the Middle English period.

2. Literature

In the early part of the Middle English period, much of the literature was written in French, though doubtless there was a continuing oral tradition in the native tongue. By the end of the twelfth century, however, some notable works in English appeared, such as the witty poem *The Owl and the Nightingale*, the verse history of Britain, the *Brut*, and a number of devotional poems. During the thirteenth century, the eclipse of English by French as the language of literature was arrested, and alongside verse romances and lyrics in English we find a beautifully wrought prose devotional guide, the *Ancrene Wisse*. In the fourteenth century, there was a surge of literary production, including the works of Chaucer, Gower, Langland and the *Gawain*-poet. In addition, there are prose meditations of mystics, religious drama, secular and religious lyrics and verse romances of adventure and the supernatural. The authorship of most of these works is unknown.

Some of the finest of these works (the works of the *Gawain*-poet and Langland's *Piers Plowman*) were written in the traditional English alliterative verse form of Anglo-Saxon times. Chaucer's favourite verse-scheme, however, was the heroic couplet, which became the staple for English verse for many centuries.

The fifteenth century is probably most notable for developments in drama, for the works of the 'Scottish Chaucerians', Henryson and

James I of Scotland, and for the great prose collection of Arthurian stories, Malory's *Morte d'Arthur*.

The language of the *Clerk's Tale*

1. Semantic change

Many Middle English words have survived virtually unchanged to the present day, and, even if spelling forms have altered, it is often quite easy to recognise the words by reading them aloud in their contexts. More difficult is detecting instances where words have undergone partial or total shifts of meaning – a process known as semantic change. When a word has completely changed, it is evident at once that the modern meaning no longer attaches to it: Walter's people kneel to him *buxomly* (line 186), Grisildis knows domestic skills through *wit* (line 428) and she gives birth to a *knave* (line 444). There is little danger of our failing to recognise drastic semantic change in these instances, when the modern renderings are 'obediently', 'knowledge' and 'boy'.

We are in danger, however, when the modern meaning of a word seems to make reasonable sense in the context. Consider the following:

- (a) Wol nat oure lord yet leve his *vanytee*? (line 250)
- (b) ... be ye redy with good herte/To al my *lust* (lines 351–2)
- (c) This markys in his herte longeth so/To tempte his wyf, hir *sadnesse* for to knowe (lines 451–2)
- (d) Nat with no swollen thoght in hire *corage* (line 950)

'Vanity', 'lust', 'sadness' and 'courage' would appear to make some kind of sense, but they would all be totally incorrect translations. 'Foolish way of life', 'wishes', 'steadfastness' and 'heart' are close modern equivalents. Thus it is wise to keep a wary eye on the glossaries even when encountering words which have identical Modern English forms.

2. 'Thou' and 'ye'

The pronouns *thou* and *ye* in fourteenth-century English could both be used for the singular mode of address and, as in Modern French *tu/ vous* and Modern German *du/Sie*, they imply different social relationships. *Thou* is used when speaking to an inferior or to express affection. *Ye* (as a singular) is used when speaking to a superior or in compliments; when *both* parties in a conversation address one another as *ye* they are almost invariably members of upper-class society.

When Petrarch wrote his tale in Latin he consistently used *tu* as the only singular form and *vos* as the plural, even though the 'plural of respect' was common in late Latin. Petrarch's French translator follows him slavishly in this respect, even to the absurd extent of having the peasant Janicula address his *seigneur* as *tu*:

> 'Riens,' dist il, 'sire, vouloir ne doy que ce qui *te* plaist, qui es mon droiturier seigneur.'

But, when Chaucer comes to describe this episode in the *Clerk's Tale*, he departs from his sources in this important detail (lines 319–21):

> 'Lord,' quod he, 'my willynge
> Is as *ye* wole, ne aveynes *youre* likynge
> I wol no thyng.'

Here, and throughout the *Clerk's Tale*, we see Chaucer consistently employing the *thou/ye* forms to indicate personal (and, on occasion, changing) relationships. The forms used by the speakers are in line with what we would expect:

Janicula addresses Walter as *ye* (superior)

Walter addresses Janicula as *thou* (inferior)

Grisildis addresses her child as *thou* (intimate)

The most interesting forms are those used between Walter and Grisildis. We know that, well before he has spoken to her, Walter has grown to admire Grisildis (lines 233–41), and this is subsequently reflected in his rather surprising use of *ye* in addressing a peasant-girl (line 297). With the exception of lines 483–9, where Walter purports to be expressing the opinions of others, he uses the polite plural of respect to Grisildis. But at line 890 he changes to *thou*. Grisildis has just asked that her smock be returned to her so that she does not have to walk naked before the people (lines 876–9). Walter is deeply moved and, for the first time, he uses *thou*.

> 'The smok,' quod he, 'that *thou* hast on *thy* bak,
> Lat it be stille, and bere it forth with *thee*.'
> But wel unnethes thilke word he spak,
> But wente his wey, for routhe and for pitee. (lines 890–3)

To Grisildis, this use of *thou* must seem a gratuitous addition to his cruel behaviour – a harsh reminder of her demotion from marchioness back to peasant. The audience knows, however, that Walter can hardly speak and has to turn away because he was overcome with pity. Poignancy is thus heightened because *thou* contains, simultaneously, the opposite potentials of intimacy and alienation. From this point on, Walter uses only the *thou* form to Grisildis, notably (fifteen times in all) when he kisses her and restores the children to her (lines 1051–78).

We thus become aware of a linguistic ambivalence which must have been clearly evident to Chaucer's audience, and have left them – as it leaves us – with two questions:

(1) Walter initially addresses Grisildis as *ye* as a mark of acceptance as a social *equal*. But is *her* employment of *ye* in addressing her husband rather a recognition of his *superiority*? She does not switch to *thou* at the end, even though he embraces her and addresses her as *thou*.

(2) What does Walter intend in that interim period between line 890 and the dénouement, when he most humiliates Grisildis, yet most pities her? Because *thou* has opposite potentials (affection/alienation) might he use *thou* because it can simultaneously both conceal and express his emotions?

It is clear that the ambivalence of *thou* adds to the psychological complexity of the story.

Perhaps, in the last analysis, such questions cannot be conclusively resolved. The cut-and-dried, the unambiguous, are not Chaucer's mode of working. Time after time, the depiction of character in his works hints only at possibilities, reflecting the uncertainties, the subtleties of human personalities and relationships. For example, the ageing Wife of Bath tells a story which poses and answers the question 'What do women most desire?' The answer is 'Domination over their husbands'. As we have seen earlier, the Clerk's story is a rebuttal of that philosophy, a direct challenge to the Wife of Bath's views. Yet at the dénouement of her tale an old woman is magically transformed to a sexually attractive girl, whose amazed husband – a young knight – then kisses her a thousand times:

And she obeyed hym in every thyng
That myghte doon hym plesance or likyng. (lines 1255–6)

Is the myth of an old woman restored to youth a projection of her own fantasies? And, in that moment of love, is there an admission ('and she *obeyed* hym') that only through mutual and equal 'obedience' can there be happiness in marriage?

Thus, though the Clerk directs his tale against the apparently entrenched opinions of the Wife of Bath, there are inconsistencies in her that betray a wistfulness and an uncertainty of belief which transform a caricature into a character. The reader senses a similar depiction of ambiguity of character in the *Clerk's Tale* when Walter, on the brink of tears and addressing Grisildis with the ambivalent *thou*, makes us hesitant about dismissing him simply as a heartless tyrant.

3. The historical present

A particular feature of fourteenth-century English is the use of the historical present (the recounting of past events in the present tense) to intensify a dramatic description. The effect is that readers find themselves in the midst of the living action rather than following an account of things past. The historical present is, of course, common in Modern English but we tend to demand consistency in sequence of tense – that is to say, if we begin a description in the historical present it is generally felt to be stylistically incorrect to drop into the preterite.

Such consistency was not felt to be necessary in Middle English and this results in a difficulty in making a translation. Consider the following examples:

> The time of undren of the same day
> *Approcheth*, that this weddyng sholde be;
> And al the paleys *put was* in array . . .   (lines 260–2)

> Thus Walter lowely – nay, but roially –
> Wedded with fortunat honestetee,
> In Goddes pees *lyveth* ful esily
> At hoom, and outward grace ynogh *had* he;   (lines 421–4)

There is little choice in translating such passages but to render them consistently in the past tense. It is unfortunate that the dramatic intensity of the first passage and the scene-setting of the second will be lost by so doing.

Study note: In this instance, as in many more, it will readily be appreciated that no translation can fully catch the subtleties of the original. If you have to change tense for the sake of consistent tense-sequence in a written translation, briefly indicate in a note that modern usage forces you to make the adjustment. You should also point out that the effects of Middle English historical present (intensifying of the drama, setting of scene) are inevitably lost in the process.

4. Tags

Chaucer frequently departs from his Latin and French sources by adding tags. Such tags, or stock phrases, were common in English rhymed popular romances, and there is little doubt that (because tags normally occur at the end of lines) Chaucer's use of them was sometimes prompted by a search for rhyme, though, on the credit side, the effect can be a heightening of the illusion of spontaneity of everyday speech. They should often be regarded as no more than that, however, and too literal a translation can give them an importance that would not have been felt by a contemporary audience, or, indeed, might endow them with meaning that could be considered inept. Consider the following examples in their contexts:

Line 67　　Walter's people readily obeyed him *bothe lasse and moore*. This literally means, 'both those in low and those in high estate'. It is a common circumlocution for 'all', and it is doubtful that the idea of social divisions was inherent in the phrase. So also *moore and lesse* (line 940).

Line 172　　Walter tells the people that he will give up his freedom by marrying but that they must accept his choice of a wife *as evere moot I thryve*, (literally, 'so may I ever thrive'). This very common tag is no more than an intensifier, such as 'indeed' or 'certainly'.

Line 371　　Walter tells the people that they must honour Grisildis, *ther is namoore to seye*. This tag recurs constantly in Chaucer's writings (several times in the *Clerk's Tale* itself) and, like *as evere moot I thryve* (above), seems to be no more than an intensifier.

Line 609　　Grisildis never mentions her lost daughter *in ernest nor in game*. It would clearly be quite out of keeping with the solemnity of this passage to translate this common phrase literally. It simply means, 'ever', or 'on any occasion'. Similarly *for ernest ne for game* (line 733).

Study note: You will find other instances of rhyme-tags similar to those discussed above. Use your judgement in each case to determine whether a literal or more general translation suits the context.

5. 'Will', 'shall' and the future tense

A particular problem in Middle English lies in the construction of the future tense. In Old English, the form of the future tense was identical to that of the present. The listener or reader would deduce the tense from the context, just as we do in Modern English when we find: *I go* [or, *I am going*] *to London tomorrow* alongside *I shall go to London tomorrow*.

When *will* was used as an auxiliary verb in Old English it implied a wish (volitional); when *shall* was used it implied an obligation. In Middle English the volitional meaning of *will* is usually present, and the sense of obligation (or of certainty of future events) is often present in *shall*. Consider the following:

1. Thy doghter *wol* I take, er that I wende (line 307)
2. Thanne *shal* the blood of Janicle succede (line 632)
3. And forthermoore, this *shal* ye swere (line 169)

In the first example, Walter is *requesting* Janicula for permission to marry Grisildis. The context makes it clear that he is not saying, 'I *will* marry your daughter', but is using the verb volitionally, 'I *wish to* marry your daughter'. In example 2, the inevitability of future occurrence is inherent in *shal* in much stronger sense than in Modern English *shall*: 'It is certain that the blood of Janicula will succeed'. In example 3, the sense of obligation is strong, 'And moreover, you *must* promise this'.

Occasionally, the auxiliary verbs *will* and *shall* simply express the future, without volitional or certainty/obligatory implication. Judge for yourself which sense seems the most likely in any given context.

The verse form of the *Clerk's Tale*

Preface: some technical terms

In the following discussion of verse form, there are inevitably some technical terms which may be new to you. This section is therefore prefaced with definitions of such terms, in the order in which they appear in the ensuing discussion:

octosyllabic line: a line of poetry made up of eight syllables, for example:

1 2 3 4 5 6 7 8
And, also domb as any stoon

iambic: a verse foot, or unit, of two syllables, the first of which is unstressed, the second stressed; for example, the line quoted above has four feet, each of which is an iamb:

| x / | x / | x / | x / |
| And, al | so domb | as an | y stoon |

couplet: a verse form where two successive lines rhyme, often followed by a different rhyme for the next two lines, for example:

Thou sittest at another book	*a*
Tyl fully daswed is thy look,	*a*
And lyvest thus as an heremyte,	*b*
Although thyn abstynence ys lyte.	*b*

The last two lines in each stanza of the *Clerk's Tale* form a couplet.

pentameter: a line of poetry made up of five feet. If the stress happens to be iambic, then such verse would be said to be written in *iambic pentameters*, for example:

$$\begin{array}{|c|c|c|c|c|}
\overset{\text{x}}{} \quad \overset{/}{} & \overset{\text{x}}{} \quad \overset{/}{} & \overset{\text{x}}{} \quad \overset{/}{} & \overset{\text{x}}{} \overset{/}{} & \overset{\text{x}}{} \quad \overset{/}{}
\end{array}$$

|̇ But took | the child | and wente | upon | his weye |̇

end-stopped: a line of poetry in which the syntactical unit (a main clause, a subordinate clause, and so on) is exactly contained and the line often ends, therefore, with a mark of punctuation indicating a natural pause. In the lines quoted under 'couplet' (above) there is end-stopping:

Thou sittest at another book (*main clause*)
Tyl fully daswed is thy look, (*subordinate adverbial clause of time*)
And lyvest thus as an heremyte, (*main clause*)
Although thyn abstinence ys lyte. (*subordinate adverbial clause of concession*)

enjambement: unlike 'end-stopped', the syntactical unit runs on from one line into the next, for example:

atte leeste
Burieth this litel body in som place

The sense ('at least bury this little body somewhere') runs straight on over the usual pause one feels at the end of a line. This often produces a feeling of tension and/or urgency.

trochee: a two-syllable verse foot, the first syllable being stressed, the second unstressed:

$$\begin{array}{|c|}
\overset{/}{} \quad \overset{\text{x}}{}
\end{array}$$

|̇ Gooth now |̇

Rhyme-royal

Chaucer's earliest poetry was written in octosyllabic lines (of basically iambic stress) rhyming in couplets (aa,bb,cc,dd, and so on). An example of this can be seen in the passage quoted from the *House of Fame* on p. 6. The bulk of his work, however, is written in iambic pentameters, and, although much of this is again in rhyming couplets, some works are in stanzaic form. Iambic couplets are used in the *General Prologue* (as in the description of the Clerk quoted on pp. 8–9) while the *Clerk's Tale* itself is in Chaucer's favourite among stanzaic forms, *rhyme-royal*, with its rhyme-scheme ababbcc. He had used rhyme-royal on a number of occasions, including the *Parliament of Fowls* and *Troilus and Criseyde*, and achieves remarkable variety of effect within the restriction of the stanza.

Rhyme-royal may be of Italian origin, but Chaucer would have been acquainted with it in some of the works of Guillaume de Machaut, his French contemporary. Even though Chaucer was able to express comic colloquial speech in this form – to be seen in the words of the duck in the *Parliament* – he generally reserves rhyme-royal for works of sober dignity. He greatly varies the divisions within each stanza, and, while the basic stress pattern is iambic, this too is fluid so that he can avoid monotony and achieve diversity of effect. Again, many lines are end-stopped, but often the syntax runs over into the next line (a device known as *enjambement*) so as to create a sense of speed or of tension between rhythm and syntax. In spite of the formality of the stanza, Chaucer marvellously preserves the natural word-order of speech.

Some of these effects can be exemplified by examining a stanza in some detail:

'Gooth now,' quod she, 'and dooth my lordes heeste;
But o thyng wol I prey yow of youre grace,
That, but my lord forbad yow, atte leeste
Burieth this litel body in som place
That beestes ne no briddes it torace.'
But he no word wol to that purpos seye,
But took the child and wente upon his weye.   (lines 568–74)

Grisildis has been told by the sergeant that she is to give her daughter to him and that he is acting under Walter's orders. Grisildis's first words reverse the iambic stress, and the trochee simultaneously lays extra emphasis on the imperative *Gooth* and confirms her total acceptance of Walter's command; the regular rhythm and end-stopping of the rest of the line reinforce this unequivocal response:

$$\overset{/}{\text{'Gooth}}\ \overset{x}{\text{now,'}}\ \Big|\ \overset{x}{\text{quod}}\ \overset{/}{\text{she,}}\ \Big|\ \overset{x}{\text{'and}}\ \overset{/}{\text{dooth}}\ \Big|\ \overset{x}{\text{my}}\ \overset{/}{\text{lor}}\ \Big|\ \overset{x}{\text{des}}\ \overset{/}{\text{heeste'}}\ \Big|$$

Having made clear her absolute compliance, however, Grisildis then ventures a request, *But . . .* Her hesitancy in urging this is reflected in the suspension between *But* and its verb, *Burieth*: first she uses a sup-pliant tone to the grim-looking sergeant (*I prey yow*) and her attri-bution of *grace* to such an evidently cruel man pitifully betrays the forlornness of the hope that she entertains. For a second time she hesi-tates lest her prayer should appear to call in question her husband's command (*but my lord forbad yow*); then the agonised request rushes through ignoring the natural pause at the end of the line in the enjambe-ment of *atte leeste/Burieth this litel body*. (So much has Grisildis hesi-tated in making her request, that she loses sight of the syntax and ends up by saying, 'But I pray you that bury this little body' – the kind of gram-matical inconsistency which is common in speech if simple sentence-structure is interrupted.) The unswervingly iambic stress of the final couplet with its repeated *But* reinforces its sense of finality: the inflexibility of the sergeant is reflected in the inflexibility of the metre:

> But he no word wol to that purpos seye,
> But took the child and wente upon his weye.

Study note: Choose some other stanzas from the *Clerk's Tale* for close analysis. Such an exercise will reveal the extraordinary variety of effect Chaucer obtains within the apparent rigidity of the stanzaic form.

Part 4

Hints for study

Understanding the language

The obvious barrier to a reading of Chaucer is linguistic. Some points of specific difficulty are discussed on pp. 44–9, but you will find that working through the text carefully a few times will enable you to build up a quite extensive vocabulary so that you can approach the poetry without consciousness of translating. Reading aloud, even if you can manage only an approximation to the pronunciation, will help both in understanding and also in appreciating the music of the poetry. French-derived words in Middle English often retain their original final-syllable stress; Germanic words (like words in Modern English) take their stress on the first syllable:

$$\left| \begin{matrix} x & / \\ \text{I have} \end{matrix} \right| \begin{matrix} x & / \\ \text{no womm} \end{matrix} \left| \begin{matrix} x / \\ \text{en su} \end{matrix} \right| \begin{matrix} x / \\ \text{ffisaunt,} \end{matrix} \left| \begin{matrix} x & / \\ \text{certayn,} \end{matrix} \right|$$ (line 960)

You will observe that the French loan-words *suffisaunt* and *certayn* are stressed as in French, whereas in Modern English their stresses are completely reversed:

$$\begin{matrix} x & / & x \\ \text{sufficient} \end{matrix} \qquad \begin{matrix} / & x \\ \text{certain} \end{matrix}$$

This is, of course, because the words have, over the centuries, been so completely adopted into English that we no longer think of them as French. Words derived from Old English should be pronounced phonetically – that is to say, all consonants should be pronounced. For example, both the *k* and the *n* in *knave* should be pronounced, just as they are in the German *Knabe*.

Checking your ability to translate

It is very easy to glide over translation problems without fully recognising their existence. Do not allow yourself to get away with a translation that 'more or less' catches the meaning. From time to time, take a stanza at random and write out a close translation of it, making sure that you account for every word of the original. It is usually expected that you translate verse into Modern English prose. If a particular Middle English idiom no longer exists in Modern English, substitute the most apt idiom you can think of – but, if you use much licence here, you should indicate in a note what the literal meaning of the original is.

Critical judgements

Listen to the views of others and read critical essays with an open mind; but in the end it is your own considered opinion that matters, provided that you can support your views with accurate knowledge, clear reasoning and apt reference to the text.

Quotation

It is worth committing to memory lines, phrases, even single words, that will help to illustrate the points you make in your essays. A bald assertion is unpersuasive. A reasoned argument, backed by carefully selected textual reference, is telling. Do not, however, substitute long passages of quotation for critical discussion: a line here, a phrase there, closely integrated into your analysis of the topic is what is required to fix and locate your argument. Naturally, some topics will require rather more quotation than others – an essay on style is more likely to include illustrative passages than a more general discussion of theme.

Do not trouble too much about the precise spelling of Middle English words. (There was, in any case, no standard spelling until later, and indeed the same word may well occur with various spellings even in the same manuscript.)

Some suggestions for essay titles

You may well wish to focus your attention on some of the main approaches to the *Clerk's Tale* in essay form. Obviously, discussion of one aspect of the tale will overlap with other aspects; this is reflected below in some repetition of 'Suggested points for consideration' topics that follow the essay titles. Neither the essay titles nor the 'points for consideration' are intended to be prescriptive or exhaustive, and you may decide to subdivide titles (b), (c) and (d) into several (shorter) essays.

(a) 'To what extent does the tale fit the teller?'

Suggested points for consideration: the description of the Clerk in the *General Prologue to the Canterbury Tales* (quoted on pp. 8–9); the education of medieval clerks (see pp. 41–2); the additions the Clerk makes to the Petrarch version; the tale-within-a-tale, notably the dialogue about marriage in the 'Marriage Group'; the prologue and epilogue to the tale; the religious, allegorical nature of the story.

(b) 'Discuss the characterisation in the *Clerk's Tale*'

Suggested points for consideration: realistic versus allegorical interpretation; Harry Bailly's reaction in the epilogue and that of the Merchant in the prologue to his tale; the Paduan versus the Veronese reactions to Petrarch's story (see p. 36), and the applicability of those opposed reactions to a consideration of the *Clerk's Tale*; Janicula; the people of Saluzzo; Walter; Grisildis.

(c) 'What can we learn about the Clerk's intentions in his story by comparing it with its sources and analogues?'

Suggested points for consideration: explain the difference between source and analogue; development of the story through folklore and the Cupid and Psyche motif of taboo; Boccaccio's version; Petrarch's version (including that of the anonymous French translator); the Clerk's additions and alterations to the Latin and French versions (see pp. 37–8); story-within-story setting; the 'moral' of the story in its various versions.

(d) 'Discuss the language, style and structure of the *Clerk's Tale*'

Suggested points for consideration: Harry Bailly's request (line 19) for plain style; does the Clerk accede to this request?; the biblical quotations and references and their significance; the poetic form (rhyme-royal) – include some detailed analyses; the story pattern; the language of Harry Bailly in the prologue and epilogue to the *Clerk's Tale* compared with that of the Clerk; linguistic usages which may not immediately be seen as significant by a modern reader, but which affect the interpretation of the tale (for example, *thou* and *ye*, see pp. 44–6).

Part 5

Suggestions for further reading

The text

Complete text of Chaucer's works

The standard complete edition of Chaucer's works (from which all quotations in the present book are taken) is F.N. Robinson (ed.), *The Complete Works of Geoffrey Chaucer*, second edition, Oxford University Press, Oxford, 1957. There are later reprints. The third, revised, edition is in preparation and will be published (probably in 1986) by Houghton Mifflin, Boston, Massachusetts, under the general editorship of L.D. Benson.

Separate editions of the Clerk's Tale

BARBER, M.M. (ED.): *The Clerk of Oxford's Tale*, Macmillan, London; St Martin's Press, New York, 1956.

SISAM, K. (ED.): *Chaucer's Clerk's Tale*, Clarendon Press, Oxford, reprinted 1949.

WINNY, J. (ED.): *Chaucer's Clerk's Tale*, Cambridge University Press, Cambridge, 1966.

Critical and biographical works

BREWER, D.S.: *Chaucer*, Longman, London, reprinted, 1973.

CROW, M.M., and OLSON, C.C. (EDS.): *Chaucer: Life-records*, Oxford University Press, Oxford, 1966.

KITTREDGE, G.L.: 'Chaucer's Discussion of Marriage', *Modern Philology*, Vol.9, 1911–12, pp. 435–67. This essay is reprinted in Shoek, R.J. and Taylor J. (eds.), *Chaucer Criticism*, Vol.1, University of Notre Dame Press, Notre Dame, Indiana, reprinted 1978, pp. 130–59; in Wagenknecht, E. (ed.), *Chaucer: Modern Essays in Criticism*, Oxford University Press, Oxford, 1959, pp. 188–215; and in Anderson, J.J. (ed.), *Chaucer: the Canterbury Tales*, Casebook series, Macmillan, London, 1977, pp. 61–92. These critical anthologies contain further essays of relevance to the *Clerk's Tale*.

ROWLAND, B. (ED.): *Companion to Chaucer Studies*, Oxford University Press, New York and Oxford, 1979. (Contains resumés and discussions of critical opinions, and also detailed bibliographies. For a discussion of the allegorical element in the *Clerk's Tale*, see R.P. Miller, 'Allegory in the *Canterbury Tales*', pp. 338–9.)

SALTER, E.: *Chaucer: The Knight's Tale and The Clerk's Tale*, Edward Arnold, London, 1962

Sources and analogues

BOCCACCIO, GIOVANNI: *The Decameron*, translated by G.H. McWilliam, Penguin Books, Harmondsworth, 1972.

BRYAN, W.F., and DEMPSTER, G. (EDS.): *Sources and Analogues of Chaucer's Canterbury Tales*, reprinted Atlantic Highlands, New Jersey, 1958. Contains the Petrarch story of Griselda, and the French translation of Petrarch, also used by Chaucer. Texts are in the original languages, with English marginal paraphrases.

CHILD, F.J. (ED.): *The English and Scottish Popular Ballads*, reprinted by the Folklore Press in association with Pageant Book Company, New York, 1957, Vol.2, Contains *Fair Annie* versions, pp. 63–83.

MASON, E. (TRANS.): *Lais of Marie de France*, Everyman's Library, Dent, London and New York, reprinted 1966. Contains *Lai le Freine*, pp. 91–101.

ROBINSON, J.H.: *Petrarch: the First Modern Scholar and Man of Letters*, G.P. Putnam's Sons, Knickerbocker Press, New York and London, 1898. See pp. 191–6 for a translation of Petrarch's letter to Boccaccio on the subject of the Griselda story.

SANDS, D.B. (ED.): *Middle English Verse Romances*, Holt, Rinehart & Winston, New York, Chicago, San Francisco, Toronto, London, 1966. Contains Middle English translation of *Le Freisne*, pp. 233–45.

Language

BAUGH, A.C.: *A History of the English Language*, Routledge & Kegan Paul, London, second revised edition, 1959.

ELLIOTT, R.W.V.: *Chaucer's English*, André Deutsch, London, 1974.

MUSTANOJA, T.F.: *A Middle English Syntax*, Société Néophilogique, Helsinki, 1960.

The author of these notes

COLIN WILCOCKSON was educated at Chigwell School and Merton College, Oxford, where he read English Language and Literature. He taught for some years at Campbell College, Belfast, and, as Senior English Master and Deputy Headmaster, at The Leys School, Cambridge. He was elected a Fellow of Pembroke College, Cambridge, where he is Director of Studies in English and Tutor for Admissions. He has published books, articles and reviews mainly on medieval subjects and on the twentieth-century poet and artist, David Jones. Most recently, he has edited the *Book of the Duchess* for the forthcoming third revised edition of *The Complete Works of Geoffrey Chaucer*, edited by F.N. Robinson.

York Notes: list of titles

CHINUA ACHEBE
A Man of the People
Arrow of God
Things Fall Apart

EDWARD ALBEE
Who's Afraid of Virginia Woolf?

ELECHI AMADI
The Concubine

ANONYMOUS
Beowulf
Everyman

JOHN ARDEN
Serjeant Musgrave's Dance

AYI KWEI ARMAH
The Beautyful Ones Are Not Yet Born

W. H. AUDEN
Selected Poems

JANE AUSTEN
Emma
Mansfield Park
Northanger Abbey
Persuasion
Pride and Prejudice
Sense and Sensibility

HONORÉ DE BALZAC
Le Père Goriot

SAMUEL BECKETT
Waiting for Godot

SAUL BELLOW
Henderson, The Rain King

ARNOLD BENNETT
Anna of the Five Towns

WILLIAM BLAKE
Songs of Innocence, Songs of Experience

ROBERT BOLT
A Man For All Seasons

ANNE BRONTË
The Tenant of Wildfell Hall

CHARLOTTE BRONTË
Jane Eyre

EMILY BRONTË
Wuthering Heights

ROBERT BROWNING
Men and Women

JOHN BUCHAN
The Thirty-Nine Steps

JOHN BUNYAN
The Pilgrim's Progress

BYRON
Selected Poems

ALBERT CAMUS
L'Etranger (The Outsider)

GEOFFREY CHAUCER
Prologue to the Canterbury Tales
The Franklin's Tale
The Knight's Tale
The Merchant's Tale
The Miller's Tale
The Nun's Priest's Tale
The Pardoner's Tale
The Wife of Bath's Tale
Troilus and Criseyde

ANTON CHEKHOV
The Cherry Orchard

SAMUEL TAYLOR COLERIDGE
Selected Poems

WILKIE COLLINS
The Moonstone
The Woman in White

SIR ARTHUR CONAN DOYLE
The Hound of the Baskervilles

WILLIAM CONGREVE
The Way of the World

JOSEPH CONRAD
Heart of Darkness
Lord Jim
Nostromo
The Secret Agent
Victory
Youth and *Typhoon*

STEPHEN CRANE
The Red Badge of Courage

BRUCE DAWE
Selected Poems

WALTER DE LA MARE
Selected Poems

DANIEL DEFOE
A Journal of the Plague Year
Moll Flanders
Robinson Crusoe

CHARLES DICKENS
A Tale of Two Cities
Bleak House
David Copperfield
Great Expectations
Hard Times
Little Dorrit
Nicholas Nickleby
Oliver Twist
Our Mutual Friend
The Pickwick Papers

EMILY DICKINSON
Selected Poems

JOHN DONNE
Selected Poems

THEODORE DREISER
Sister Carrie

GEORGE ELIOT
Adam Bede
Middlemarch
Silas Marner
The Mill on the Floss

T. S. ELIOT
Four Quartets
Murder in the Cathedral
Selected Poems
The Cocktail Party
The Waste Land

J. G. FARRELL
The Siege of Krishnapur

GEORGE FARQUHAR
The Beaux Stratagem

WILLIAM FAULKNER
Absalom, Absalom!
As I Lay Dying
Go Down, Moses
The Sound and the Fury

HENRY FIELDING
Joseph Andrews
Tom Jones

F. SCOTT FITZGERALD
Tender is the Night
The Great Gatsby

E. M. FORSTER
A Passage to India
Howards End

ATHOL FUGARD
Selected Plays

JOHN GALSWORTHY
Strife

MRS GASKELL
North and South

WILLIAM GOLDING
Lord of the Flies
The Inheritors
The Spire

OLIVER GOLDSMITH
She Stoops to Conquer
The Vicar of Wakefield

ROBERT GRAVES
Goodbye to All That

GRAHAM GREENE
Brighton Rock
The Heart of the Matter
The Power and the Glory

THOMAS HARDY
Far from the Madding Crowd
Jude the Obscure
Selected Poems
Tess of the D'Urbervilles
The Mayor of Casterbridge
The Return of the Native
The Trumpet Major
The Woodlanders
Under the Greenwood Tree

L. P. HARTLEY
The Go-Between
The Shrimp and the Anemone

NATHANIEL HAWTHORNE
The Scarlet Letter

SEAMUS HEANEY
Selected Poems

ERNEST HEMINGWAY
A Farewell to Arms
For Whom the Bell Tolls
The African Stories
The Old Man and the Sea

GEORGE HERBERT
Selected Poems

HERMANN HESSE
Steppenwolf

BARRY HINES
Kes

HOMER
The Iliad

ANTHONY HOPE
The Prisoner of Zenda

GERARD MANLEY HOPKINS
Selected Poems

WILLIAM DEAN HOWELLS
The Rise of Silas Lapham

RICHARD HUGHES
A High Wind in Jamaica

THOMAS HUGHES
Tom Brown's Schooldays

ALDOUS HUXLEY
Brave New World

HENRIK IBSEN
A Doll's House
Ghosts
Hedda Gabler

HENRY JAMES
Daisy Miller
The Europeans
The Portrait of a Lady
The Turn of the Screw
Washington Square

SAMUEL JOHNSON
Rasselas

BEN JONSON
The Alchemist
Volpone

JAMES JOYCE
A Portrait of the Artist as a Young Man
Dubliners

JOHN KEATS
Selected Poems

RUDYARD KIPLING
Kim

D. H. LAWRENCE
Sons and Lovers
The Rainbow
Women in Love

CAMARA LAYE
L'Enfant Noir

HARPER LEE
To Kill a Mocking-Bird

LAURIE LEE
Cider with Rosie

THOMAS MANN
Tonio Kröger

CHRISTOPHER MARLOWE
Doctor Faustus
Edward II

ANDREW MARVELL
Selected Poems

W. SOMERSET MAUGHAM
Of Human Bondage
Selected Short Stories

J. MEADE FALKNER
Moonfleet

HERMAN MELVILLE
Billy Budd
Moby Dick

THOMAS MIDDLETON
Women Beware Women

THOMAS MIDDLETON and WILLIAM ROWLEY
The Changeling

ARTHUR MILLER
Death of a Salesman
The Crucible

JOHN MILTON
Paradise Lost I & II
Paradise Lost IV & IX
Selected Poems

V. S. NAIPAUL
A House for Mr Biswas

SEAN O'CASEY
Juno and the Paycock
The Shadow of a Gunman

GABRIEL OKARA
The Voice

EUGENE O'NEILL
Mourning Becomes Electra

GEORGE ORWELL
Animal Farm
Nineteen Eighty-four

JOHN OSBORNE
Look Back in Anger

WILFRED OWEN
Selected Poems

ALAN PATON
Cry, The Beloved Country

THOMAS LOVE PEACOCK
Nightmare Abbey and Crotchet Castle

HAROLD PINTER
The Birthday Party
The Caretaker

PLATO
The Republic

ALEXANDER POPE
Selected Poems

THOMAS PYNCHON
The Crying of Lot 49

SIR WALTER SCOTT
Ivanhoe
Quentin Durward
The Heart of Midlothian
Waverley

PETER SHAFFER
The Royal Hunt of the Sun

WILLIAM SHAKESPEARE
A Midsummer Night's Dream
Antony and Cleopatra
As You Like It
Coriolanus
Cymbeline
Hamlet
Henry IV Part I
Henry IV Part II
Henry V
Julius Caesar
King Lear
Love's Labour's Lost
Macbeth
Measure for Measure
Much Ado About Nothing
Othello
Richard II
Richard III
Romeo and Juliet
Sonnets
The Merchant of Venice
The Taming of the Shrew
The Tempest
The Winter's Tale
Troilus and Cressida
Twelfth Night
The Two Gentlemen of Verona

GEORGE BERNARD SHAW
Androcles and the Lion
Arms and the Man
Caesar and Cleopatra
Candida
Major Barbara
Pygmalion
Saint Joan
The Devil's Disciple

MARY SHELLEY
Frankenstein

PERCY BYSSHE SHELLEY
Selected Poems

RICHARD BRINSLEY SHERIDAN
The School for Scandal
The Rivals

WOLE SOYINKA
The Lion and the Jewel
The Road
Three Short Plays

EDMUND SPENSER
The Faerie Queene (Book I)

JOHN STEINBECK
Of Mice and Men
The Grapes of Wrath
The Pearl

LAURENCE STERNE
A Sentimental Journey
Tristram Shandy

ROBERT LOUIS STEVENSON
Kidnapped
Treasure Island
Dr Jekyll and Mr Hyde

TOM STOPPARD
Professional Foul
Rosencrantz and Guildenstern are Dead

JONATHAN SWIFT
Gulliver's Travels

JOHN MILLINGTON SYNGE
The Playboy of the Western World

TENNYSON
Selected Poems

W. M. THACKERAY
Vanity Fair

DYLAN THOMAS
Under Milk Wood

EDWARD THOMAS
Selected Poems

FLORA THOMPSON
Lark Rise to Candleford

J. R. R. TOLKIEN
The Hobbit
The Lord of the Rings

CYRIL TOURNEUR
The Revenger's Tragedy

ANTHONY TROLLOPE
Barchester Towers

MARK TWAIN
Huckleberry Finn
Tom Sawyer

VIRGIL
The Aeneid

VOLTAIRE
Candide

EVELYN WAUGH
Decline and Fall
A Handful of Dust

JOHN WEBSTER
The Duchess of Malfi
The White Devil

H. G. WELLS
The History of Mr Polly
The Invisible Man
The War of the Worlds

ARNOLD WESKER
Chips with Everything
Roots

PATRICK WHITE
Voss

OSCAR WILDE
The Importance of Being Earnest

TENNESSEE WILLIAMS
The Glass Menagerie

VIRGINIA WOOLF
To the Lighthouse

WILLIAM WORDSWORTH
Selected Poems

W. B. YEATS
Selected Poems

Yorks Handbooks: list of titles

YORK HANDBOOKS form a companion series to York Notes and are designed to meet the wider needs of students of English and related fields. Each volume is a compact study of a given subject area, written by an authority with experience in communicating the essential ideas to students of all levels.

AN INTRODUCTORY GUIDE TO ENGLISH LITERATURE
by MARTIN STEPHEN

PREPARING FOR EXAMINATIONS IN ENGLISH LITERATURE
by NEIL McEWAN

EFFECTIVE STUDYING
by STEVE ROBERTSON *and* DAVID SMITH

THE ENGLISH NOVEL
by IAN MILLIGAN

ENGLISH POETRY
by CLIVE T. PROBYN

STUDYING CHAUCER
by ELISABETH BREWER

STUDYING SHAKESPEARE
by MARTIN STEPHEN *and* PHILIP FRANKS

AN A·B·C OF SHAKESPEARE
by P. C. BAYLEY

STUDYING MILTON
by GEOFFREY M. RIDDEN

STUDYING CHARLES DICKENS
by K. J. FIELDING

STUDYING THOMAS HARDY
by LANCE ST JOHN BUTLER

ENGLISH LITERATURE FROM THE THIRD WORLD
by TREVOR JAMES

ENGLISH USAGE
by COLIN G. HEY

ENGLISH GRAMMAR
by LORETO TODD

STYLE IN ENGLISH PROSE
by NEIL McEWAN

AN INTRODUCTION TO LITERARY CRITICISM
by RICHARD DUTTON

A DICTIONARY OF LITERARY TERMS
by MARTIN GRAY

READING THE SCREEN
An Introduction to Film Studies
by JOHN IZOD